Untying the Apron Strings: Anti-Sexist Provision for the Under-Fives

Edited by
NAIMA BROWNE
and
PAULINE FRANCE

OPEN UNIVERSITY PRESS

Milton Keynes · *Philadelphia*

Open University Press
Celtic Court
22 Ballmoor
Buckingham MK18 1XW

and
1900 Frost Road, Suite 101
Bristol, PA 19007, USA

First Published 1986
Reprinted 1989, 1992

British Library Cataloguing in Publication Data
Untying the apron strings: anti-sexist
 provision for the under-fives. –
 (Gender and education)
 1. Nursery schools – Great Britain
 2. Sex discrimination in education –
 Great Britain
 I. Browne, Naima   II. France, Pauline
 III. Series
 372'.216   LB1140.25.G7

 ISBN 0-335-15232-5

Library of Congress Cataloging in Publication Data
Untying the apron strings.
 (Gender and education series)
 Bibliography: p.
 Includes index.
 1. Nursery schools – Great Britain.   2. Sexism in
preschool education – Great Britain. I. Browne, Naima.
II. France, Pauline.   III. Series.
LB1140.25.G7U58 1986   372'.216'0941   86-5102
ISBN 0-335-15232-5 (pbk.)

Typeset by Rowland Phototypesetting Limited
Bury St Edmunds, Suffolk
Printed in Great Britain by St Edmundsbury Press
Bury St Edmunds, Suffolk

OPEN UNIVERSITY PRE~
Gender and Education Se~

Editors
ROSEMARY DEEM~
Senior Lecturer in the School of Education a
Open University
GABY WEINER
Principal Lecturer in Education at
South Bank Polytechnic

The series provides compact and clear accounts of relevant research and practice in the field of gender and education. It is aimed at trainee and practising teachers, and parents and others with an educational interest in ending gender inequality. All age-ranges will be included, and there will be an emphasis on ethnicity as well as gender. Series authors are all established educational practitioners or researchers.

CONTENTS

Nursery education is one of the most neglected parts of the British schooling system. Starved of funds, as Naima Browne points out in Chapter 2, it is also neglected in the considerations of educational policy-makers. Surprisingly little has been made of the importance of the earliest stages of schooling in the continuing debate about how best to develop anti-sexist and anti-racist school practice, perhaps because feminist nursery workers are too busy trying to work miracles in their classrooms (see Anita Preston, Chapter 9).

The appearance of this book, the third in the Gender and Education Series, is particularly timely. It is written by women very involved in the pre-school movement: parents, researchers, teachers, community workers or combinations of these. The contributors have chosen a variety of starting-points from which to challenge the traditional practice of nurseries, drawing on the historical, the comparative, the practical and the polemic. All agree that sexual inequality provides one of the major obstacles to a genuinely egalitarian schooling system.

The first three chapters (by Naima Browne, Pauline France and Sue Duxbury) provide an important background to the current condition of the nursery school. We need reminding that there is a strong tradition of pre-school provision in Britain (at the turn of the century, just over 40 per cent of all 3- to 5-year-olds spent some time in school), though there is scant evidence of it today. Sue Duxbury shows that Britain has a very weak record compared with the rest of Europe. In 1982 we lost 1,000 nursery schools, in contrast to the European trend to extend nursery provision.

The other chapters in the book focus on the theoretical, institutional and practical implications of anti-sexist and anti-racist practice in nurseries today: how children develop gender identity and stereotypical attitudes (Chapter 4); practical guidance for teachers from a parent on how to develop co-operation between home and school (Chapter 5); the forms of pre-school provision most appropriate for children and parents (Chapter 6); reflections on a study of the attitudes of staff in two nursery classes (Chapter 7); the importance of reviewing and evaluating learning resources used in the nursery (Chapter 8); and a strong practical statement about the issues feminist nursery workers necessarily confront in their everyday lives and strategies they have developed to take feminist ideas forward (Chapter 9).

This book will be of considerable relevance to anyone interested in gender issues in education. It will also be of interest to any parent with pre-school-age children and particularly useful for feminist nursery workers, who will surely find political sustenance and sisterly support as well as practical guidance within these pages.

Rosemary Deen
Gaby Weiner

ACKNOWLEDGEMENTS

We should like to thank the following people for their support and help with the preparation of this book: Phil Browne, Rosemary Deem, Kiran Neilson, Neil Parr and Gaby Weiner. We would also like to thank all the contributors, who have worked so hard.

Naima Browne has taught for several years in Inner London schools and was an advisory nursery teacher based at the ILEA's Centre for Urban Educational Studies. She has organized workshops for nursery and infant teachers on anti- and non-sexist teaching strategies. She is currently researching into the educational provision made for very young children in nineteenth-century London.

Sue Duxbury is a nursery teacher on Merseyside and has recently completed research on working-class women with pre-school children.

Naomi Eisenstadt, an American, has lived in Britain for eleven years. She worked in various under-fives centres in Britain before setting up Moorland Children's Centre in February 1978. Since June 1983 she has been working on the Education for Family Life project at the Open University. This project has published materials for teachers to facilitate discussions of family relationships in the classroom. She has one son, aged four.

Pauline France has been a teacher in nursery, infant and junior schools in London and for five years was an advisory teacher at the ILEA's Centre for Urban Educational Studies. During this time she directed an action research project focusing on the development of approaches and materials that support the language and learning of bilingual under-fives in the nursery classroom. She has a young son and is currently involved in a co-operatively run neighbourhood nursery.

Minnie Kumria came to Britain from India in 1972. Since then she has been involved in the specialized bookselling of black literature. She is a director and manager of Soma Books Ltd at the Commonwealth Institute, London. For the last few years she has been involved in giving talks on Asian culture, black women in Britain, black women in publishing and the generation gap among Asians in Britain.

Anita Preston is an ILEA nursery teacher. She has a scale post for home–school liaison. She was liberated in the late 1960s by the women's movement and the playgroup movement, and has been involved in under-fives work in a variety of roles ever since. She is a member of the London Rape Crisis Collective, and is an ILEA school governor. She has three grown-up children and a new baby.

Glen Thomas has taught for twenty-five years. She spent a number of years working with young children with special needs. Whilst studying part-time for a degree in Education, she became interested in the issue of sexism in education. She decided to focus on the nursery for her study, as she wanted to extend her experience. She lives and works in London and has two teenage children.

CHAPTER 1

Untying the Apron Strings: Introduction

NAIMA BROWNE AND PAULINE FRANCE

It is our belief that sexism is all too pervasive in British society. Indeed, society is structured in a way that is discriminatory against females. Those women who have achieved have done so only by assuming the role of 'honorary male'. They have had in fact to be better than some males to take on this role – better qualified, more articulate, more aggressive, more stamina, more patience – yet remaining feminine and non-threatening (a formula spelt out by Constance Carroll in Hull *et al.* 1982).

Sexism operates at all levels in the daily lives of women and girls. It is manifested in the actions and behaviour of others, in the visual representation of the sexes and in the way language is used to differentiate between the sexes and to trivialize the experience and skills of females. Women in Britain who care for young children are particularly susceptible. We have noted before how forcefully language is used to uphold a predominantly heterosexual patriarchal society, by 'reminding' girls and women of their responsibilities to their home, children and menfolk (Browne and France 1985). Over a period of time we observed and analysed the language used by nursery workers, including ourselves, to young children and discovered clear patterns of sex differentiation.

We have come across one popular phrase that we feel sums up conventional attitudes towards the role of women and the relationship they must have with their (male) children; this is, 'tied to his mother's apron strings'. This phrase makes us uneasy on two counts. Firstly, the assumption is that the mother will have a domestic, servicing role, and that she needs the metaphoric apron to keep her clean while she cooks, cleans, scrubs, polishes, bathes, changes nappies, does the gardening and hangs wallpaper. Secondly, the phrase is used as a criticism of a close relationship between mother and child (never father and child). Yet there is a tremendous pressure on mothers, highlighted by the child-care 'experts', to bond with their babies and very young infants:

> Properly protected by her man, the mother is saved from having to turn outwards to deal with her surroundings at the time when she is wanting so much to turn inwards, when she is longing to be concerned with the inside of the circle which she can make with her arms, in the centre of which is the baby.
>
> (Winnicott 1967)

However, it seems that once children become part of a nursery institution there is a drive to distance mothers from the caring and educating process, particularly mothers of boys. Boys are expected to be outward going, tough, aggressive and independent.

In planning this book we wanted to consider how women can 'untie the apron strings' that have become a symbol of the constraining domestic role traditionally associated with motherhood. We also wanted to focus on how society has set about 'untying the apron strings' between women and their children by creating a professional child-care industry. This industry neither draws on the expertise of young children's principal carers nor lends support (in terms of flexible and extended day care) to women who wish to undertake paid employment. We wanted to examine how conventional under-fives care and education have helped to 'tie the apron strings' on girls, with a covert and overt reinforcement of society's need to train a future generation

of unpaid carers. We also wanted to offer our own suggestions on how these apron strings could be untied.

All of these points have been taken up in more detail by
the writers in this book. Our contributors are all women
who have had direct and recent experience of pre-school
provision in Britain, some as parents of young children,
some as workers in the field. Our discussions have highlighted a number of issues including the complex relationship between anti-sexist and anti-racist education,
and it is these issues that we want to touch on here.

There has been a good deal of debate about the similarities and differences between anti-sexist and anti-racist
education. Parallels have been drawn between the struggle
for an educational system that does not undervalue and
subsequently alienate black children and the efforts by
feminists to get a fairer deal for girls. The education of both
groups takes place in a patriarchal society where white
males hold sway. Yet conflicts between a commitment to
anti-racist education and allegiance to anti-sexist education
have been identified. Interestingly enough most writers
who point to conflicts are either white feminists or black
males, who seem to prefer a commitment to one or the
other; black feminists do not seem to have such split
allegiances.[1]

There are differences between anti-sexist and anti-racist
education. Although each has developed as an attempt to
help children to develop 'human' values and respect for
others, to have high aspirations and not underestimate
themselves, and to become aware of, understand and
confront the prejudices that are woven into the social fabric,
these prejudices operate in very different ways:

> Race, ethnic and sex prejudice are complex phenom-
> ena. . . . These prejudices stem from different economic,
> social and emotional conditions and events. They differ in
> intensity, pervasiveness, degree of reality distortion and
> extent of emotional charge. Non-sexist and non-racist
> education . . . are [both] education but they do not stress
> the same knowledge or necessarily teach the same skills.
> (Bowman 1978)

For instance, young white girls are not as a matter of course likely to experience harassment and abuse from other girls, or to see their family treated violently by other members of the 'community'. Yet this is the experience of black children, both girls and boys, growing up in Britain. There are still nursery staff who view children from cultural and linguistic backgrounds different from their own as culturally and linguistically deprived, and they let this view shape their teaching and classroom organization; by contrast young girls, on the whole, are not treated as culturally and linguistically deprived and in need of remediation. (It may be argued, however, that cultural deprivation does start for girls in a classroom where they are expected to take on a narrow stereotyped role, and have lower expectations and less adult attention than their male peers.)

White girls and women are generally accepted as an integral part of British society, unlike black females and males, who are made to feel unwelcome newcomers by some white people. Hence the persistent use of 'immigrant' even to describe children born in Britain. Nevertheless many females in Britain are put in a subordinate role to males and are turned into victims of male violence and discriminatory legislation, subjected to half-baked theories about biologically determined lower IQs, physical abilities, different ranges of emotional capability and so on.

It is important to recognize, as Minnie Kumria points out in Chapter 5, that women in nearly every culture are treated in different ways to men. Even so, it is the right of all women to seek their own liberation without being patronized by women of other cultures who think they can do it for them.[2]

In the context of what we can hope to achieve in multi-ethnic schools and institutions, we must find ways of changing the overall patterns of discrimination and differentiation that exist; such establishments will otherwise continue to perpetuate a white male meritocracy. Nursery workers committed to a policy of anti-sexism and anti-racism must try hard to involve parents in the development of such policy, at both the theoretical and practical level.

Ways to achieve this objective are offered by some writers in the book.

Any discussion of anti-sexist nursery provision needs to take into account the political nature of decisions about the care and education of young children. Under-fives have no political power and yet they have proved to be a useful political tool. Chapter 2 shows how successive governments have adopted the view that 'in a good home the mother is the person who takes responsibility for the care and protection of her children' (Ministry of Education 1946). This view of the role of mothers in the care of the under-fives has enabled nursery provision to be used by governments in attempts to control employment patterns, particularly women's employment. Governments have in addition been able to justify cuts in public spending or nursery facilities by perfecting a selective approach to child-care theories and research findings, focusing on those areas that are politically expedient (e.g. maternal deprivation) whilst ignoring or misrepresenting others. The Jacksons' work on child-minding in 1979 failed to be taken up as a justification for increased public spending on under-fives in order to improve the situation, despite their assertion that child-minding is 'a universal and necessary consequence of the way we live now'. Instead their findings resulted in an official reaffirmation of the view that if mothers stayed at home problems would not occur (Dally 1982).

The current situation is described in Chapter 3. In comparison with other countries Britain has a very poor record of state-provided nursery facilities. Inadequacies in the state provision have resulted in the development of the private and voluntary sectors. Various contributors discuss the shortcomings of the different forms of nursery facilities; it emerges that so long as politicians regard it as legitimate to use young children as political pawns, nursery provision in Britain is going to continue to be piecemeal, inadequate, expensive and founded less on the consideration of young children's and their parents' needs than on economics.

It is paradoxical that whilst mothers have been allocated

the role of the natural and ideal care-giver, women's expertise, knowledge and experience are constantly undermined
by 'experts' (usually male) on child care. In this same vein,
training courses for nursery workers continue to suggest
that parental (which usually means maternal) involvement
is to be encouraged in nurseries – not because of what these
women have to offer to the children and the workers in the
nursery, but because it enables professionals to educate
parents on how best to bring up their children. Objections
to such a deficit view of parents are raised in Chapters 5 and
6. Not all parents, however, are able to become involved in
their child's nursery life, and to assume that 'good' parents
should is to return once more to the view that women have
no life other than that relating to their child. We say
'women', since it is rarely commented on if a father never
appears in his child's nursery.

In addition to the general effect that sexist attitudes have
on nursery provision, this book is concerned with the effect
on young children of more direct and everyday experiences
of sexism, firstly through societal pressures on parents.
These may result, for example, in anxiety if children do not
conform to the 'norms' for their gender. Children are
exposed to a whole range of influences at home, and these
are discussed in Chapter 4. Sex-role differences are not
biologically determined but begin to develop from the time
a child is born. Once in a nursery, children become subject
to the influence of their peers and also to the attitudes and
expectations of the nursery workers. In Chapter 7 Glen
Thomas describes how it is possible to become more
aware of one's own sexism and offers some reasons why
she believes this self-evaluation is important. Children
are trained to notice similarities and differences, and in
Chapter 8 we argue that one aim of education is to enable
children to think critically and be aware of the world around
them, and to help them begin to make judgements based on
reason rather than on prejudice. By focusing on one aspect
of nursery provision – the effect of visual images – we offer
possible strategies that could be used in an attempt to
provide an anti-sexist environment. In the final chapter

Anita Preston provides an encouraging account of what is possible in a school committed to anti-sexism. She points out that a nursery class is part of the primary school, and so it is not sufficient for nursery workers to concern themselves solely with the nursery; they must also work with their colleagues to develop an anti-sexist policy for the whole school.

Notes

1. Further discussion of 'conflicts' and criticisms of the white feminist movement can be found in Hemmings 1980, Amos and Parmar 1981, Hull *et al.* 1982, Bourne 1983, Brah and Minhas 1985, Foster 1985. The United States experience is discussed in Hooks 1982.
2. Some writers have clearly shown that the image of all black women being oppressed by black men is a racist stereotype and an insult to the numerous females who are opposing sexism in their daily lives: Wilson 1978, Amos and Parmar 1981, Moraga and Anzaldua 1981, Hooks 1982, Brah and Minhas 1985.

CHAPTER 2

Do the gentlemen in Whitehall know best? An historical perspective of pre-school provision in Britain

NAIMA BROWNE

Women have always been an important part of Britain's work-force, and the phenomenon of the working mother is not new. The need for care of very young children outside the home has been an issue since the Industrial Revolution. It is very disappointing then that more than 150 years later an adequate system of child-care provision has still not been developed. Disappointing but not surprising, when one examines the various trends in child care and the attitudes towards motherhood that have gained currency during the past century and a half.

This chapter traces the development of state-aided nursery facilities from the nineteenth century until the 1970s. It briefly charts the growth of some alternatives (e.g. child-minding and playgroups) and highlights possible reasons for the inadequate provision available today.

Victorian and Edwardian working mothers

The ideal of Victorian woman as a decorative, docile, delicate and dependent wife and mother was something only the wealthy could hope to approach. To a vast number of women the notion of work as degrading was irrelevant in their daily struggle to provide food and shelter for themselves and their families. In addition, the view that poverty was the result of the sufferers' own improvidence led to the comfortably off concluding that gainful employment was the only morally correct remedy for the problem. The result was that women of the leisured classes had time to grow bored with their dependent and idle existences as they supervised their array of domestic servants, nursery-maids and nannies. Meanwhile, many of their poorer sisters were struggling under 'a burden of combined household and industrial toil far too heavy for any human creature' (Black 1915).

In the nineteenth and early twentieth centuries different areas had varying traditions of working-class female employment. In Staffordshire, for example, a working-class woman was expected to work and was 'looked upon as lazy unless she took her share in contributing to the family income' (Thompson 1977). In contrast, paid employment was an impossibility for many other working-class women, regardless of the economic situation of the family. With no domestic help and no household gadgets, the job of ensuring that the male bread-winner and the children were cared for was exhausting and time-consuming, leaving little time or energy for anything else (Thompson 1977, Liddington and Norris 1984).

The status and role of middle-class women were to change in the late nineteenth and early twentieth centuries. With better education and slightly improved job opportunities, more single middle-class women went out to work. The position of married middle-class women remained unchanged, however; the majority stayed at home and supervised the household.

Given the number of women in paid employment, childcare provision was obviously needed. A possible explanation for the failure of many early feminists to campaign for it to the same degree as they campaigned for equality in education and political life lies in the very different experiences of the working classes and the upper and middle classes. There is evidence of working-class women being involved in political activity and campaigning for women's rights (Liddington and Norris 1984), but the feminists who were most visible to the policy-makers at the turn of the century were generally from the more privileged sections of society. These women had the time, opportunity and energy to campaign for women's rights. They were not tied to a job or to the home and family; to them 'womanhood was the great fact in [their] life; wifehood and motherhood but incidental relations' (Stanton and Anthony 1981). Such women could employ nannies and housekeepers to attend to the domestic sphere. Child care was not a problem for them, whereas the legal and political inequality of women was.

That women were by nature responsible for child care was an accepted view in the nineteenth and early twentieth centuries. 'The care of children in their infancy is one of the grand duties annexed to the female character by nature,' stated the feminist Mary Wollstonecraft in 1792. It is not surprising that whilst upper- and middle-class mothers engaged other women to care for their children, in working-class families the responsibility for child care fell to the mother. Some employed working-class women were fortunate enough to have parents or other relatives willing to lend a hand, and a few were able to send their child to a nursery or crèche. The rest had to be content with arrangements that were inconvenient for themselves and unsatisfactory for the child. One woman, for example, employed in the heavy, unhealthy and dangerous occupation of chain-making, worked in a shed complete with forge and anvil: 'From a pole which ran across the room there dangled a tiny swing chair for the baby, so that whilst working her hammers she could rock the child' (Sherard 1897).

If the mother was unable to enlist the help of relatives to mind her children, she often found that a large proportion of her meagre wages went on child care, a situation familiar to many women today. One such woman earning 11 shillings (55p) for four days' work had to pay 4 shillings and 8 pence (24p) to a neighbour to care for her two small children. Another woman earning a similar wage who also had two children sent one to a crèche for 4 pence a day but was forced to make alternative and more expensive arrangements for the younger child as 'he was not himself welcome there [at the crèche] because he would not accept his food from a bottle but insisted on a spoon' (Black 1915).

Women who worked from home still experienced problems if they also had young children to care for. Then, as now, homeworkers' wages were even lower than those received by factory workers, so the possibility of earning sufficient to pay for child care was further diminished. The children were a constant distraction, with the result that women tried to 'get back lost time, lost during the day in maternal duties, by nightwork' (Black 1915).

During the nineteenth and early twentieth centuries, therefore, whilst the more privileged sections of society had few worries about child care, their poorer sisters were struggling.

And so to school

Many working parents eased the problem of day care for their under-fives by sending them to school. Schools for 'infants' (children from 18 months to 7 years old) first made their appearance in England in the nineteenth century. The philanthropists responsible for the establishment of such schools were concerned with the 'rescue' of the infant, especially their moral rescue. They were alarmed by the sight of infant poor, 'herding together in larger or smaller companies, with evidence of moral turpitude ripening into habits the most disgusting' (Pole 1823). The early champions of infant schools also recognized their value to working mothers, who would not need to worry about their children (Wilderspin 1824). This view of infant schools was echoed in decades to come (see HMI reports from the mid-nineteenth century onwards).

Infant schools were not always as popular with the working classes as the philanthropic middle classes felt they ought to be. One reason for their unpopularity was the heavily middle-class-orientated value system that operated in them. Instead of using these schools, many working-class parents sent their children from the age of eighteen months to working-class private schools, the much maligned 'dame' schools. Not only did these working-class private schools have the advantage of being a community resource with all that this entailed – shared values, closeness to home, etc. They were also more flexible than the infant schools, enabling parents to send their children at whatever time of day and whenever they wanted instead of having to conform to the rules and regulations of the infant schools, which reflected their middle-class origins (Gardner 1984).

From the mid-nineteenth century onwards, kindergartens or nurseries for middle-class children were increasing in popularity (Whitbread 1972). In these the underlying aim was education, whereas the infant school continued to be concerned with the physical and moral protection of young children.

As the century wore on, working-class private schools were increasingly attacked by officialdom, and many were closed down by local authorities on grounds of inefficiency. Towards the end of the nineteenth century parents began to move away from using working-class private schools, influenced by a number of factors including the abolition of public infant-school fees, the introduction of compulsory schooling for children over the age of five and a changing attitude towards the educational benefits of schools (Roberts 1972). The result was a rise in the number of under-fives in elementary schools towards the end of the nineteenth century, until in 1900–1, 43.1 per cent of children aged 3 to 5 years were attending state schools (Roberts 1972). Sixty-eight years later Plowden was to recommend the same percentage as that needing to be catered for in state-aided nurseries.

In pre-school provision, the dichotomy of purpose along

class lines continued into the twentieth century. The provision for middle-class children concentrated on 'education', while that for working-class children emphasized 'rescue' from inadequate homes and environments. For example, the high number of young children in the 'babies' classes' in elementary schools caused concern; as a result of an inquiry in 1905 by a group of school inspectors it was clearly stated that

> a new form of school is necessary for poor children. The better parents should be discouraged from sending their children before five, whilst the poorer who must do so should send them to nursery schools rather than schools of instruction.
>
> (Board of Education 1905)

Two years later the public provision of early education and training, for all children whose home conditions and parental care were 'inadequate', was again recommended (Board of Education 1907).

Besides the difficulties presented by vague value-laden terms such as 'better parents' and 'inadequate', it is clear that in the first decade of the twentieth century state-provided nursery facilities were still seen as necessary only for children from poor homes where mothers were forced for economic reasons to work or where the conditions were a danger to health. Such a view has lingered until the present day, as is evident from the current criteria governing the allocation of day-nursery places (Garland and White 1980).

Commitment to nursery provision remained at the level of rhetoric. Whilst many local authorities began to refuse under-fives admission to elementary schools, few provided any alternative. Children from 'better' homes were probably cared for by a nurse or by their mother if she did not need (in economic terms) to work. Children and mothers from 'poorer' homes had to rely on family, neighbours and friends for support, or pay for alternative and probably more expensive pre-school facilities. From 1900 to 1910 the proportion of children aged 3 to 5 years attending school dropped dramatically to 22.7 per cent (Roberts 1972).

The early twentieth century

Policy-makers may have held back from enabling the development of nursery provision, through the allocation of
money, due to an ambivalent attitude towards working
mothers and the 'child's place'. At the turn of the century
many felt that married women who worked were a cause of
much ill-health in families. The extent of ill-health amongst
the poorer sections of society had been forcibly brought
to the policy-makers' attention by the appalling physical
condition of would-be recruits for the Boer War in 1899.

To some it was clear that 'anaemic delinquents' were the
direct outcome when 'the mother is nine or ten hours a day,
even sometimes twelve hours, away from her home in the
factory' – John Burns MP, 1906. In contrast to this, an
analysis of infant deaths in Leicester in 1895 had led others
to the conclusion that there was 'no evidence to prove that
the married woman who goes out to work is less careful of
her own and her family's well-being than are other women'
(Black 1915). Clementina Black also highlighted the double
standards that operated regarding women from different
social classes:

> In well-to-do classes of society it is a matter of course to
> employ paid help and service for young children, whether
> the mother has a profession to occupy her or not. . . . it is
> unreasonable that in one class [i.e. the working class]
> women should be bitterly blamed for finding a substitute for
> the nursery work while in another such action is regarded as
> quite normal.
>
> (1915)

During the early twentieth century a wider range of
occupations became available for women. For example,
between 1904 and 1914 there was a 110-per-cent increase in
the number of female commercial clerks. By August 1914,
3.2 million women (almost half the number of men) were
employed in industry and commerce (Roberts 1977).

The First World War resulted in a further increase in the
number of women in employment, and they were encouraged to work for the country's sake. By the end of the war,

the number of women at work was almost 5 million, with 642,000 employed in government factories and engineering works. However, although by 1918 almost 2 million women were directly replacing men, the pre-war Practices Act made it crystal clear that this replacement was only temporary, and at the end of hostilities the jobs were to be 'given back' to the returning heroes (Oakley 1981).

Despite the drive to get women working, especially in the munitions factories, very little was done by the state to provide child-care facilities for mothers engaged in war work. London County Council was the only public authority to accept responsibility for the children of war workers; and even then the LCC stressed that the offer in 1914 of a site for the MacMillan sisters to extend their nursery facilities was temporary, as was the grant of ninepence a day for the children of war workers (Blackstone 1971). Legislation making the likelihood of such provision more general was not passed until 1918.

The First World War did not have any lasting effects regarding child-care provision. This is not surprising in view of the attitudes towards women war workers, the lack of subsidized child-care provision and the reactionary tone of the press after the war. The latter stressed the view that every woman could and should be supported by a man, and any woman who continued to work did so out of 'deliberate wickedness' (Strachey 1978).

Between the Wars

Between 1918 and 1930 a number of trends were evident. More middle-class women were pursuing careers, and women generally had gained a degree of confidence, having survived years without the constant protection of their menfolk (Roberts 1977). More job opportunities for working-class women were arising, and more women were opting for public service rather than domestic service. Unfortunately women failed to use their newly achieved political power (gained by the extension of the franchise) to fight for women's issues at home. Instead they turned their attention to general issues such as world peace and improved health care. In addition, this was a time of economic uncertainty.

Against this backcloth was a series of false starts as regards nursery provision. First came the 1918 Education Act, which empowered local authorities to provide nurseries. Little enthusiasm was shown by the local authorities, since nursery provision would have necessitated a rise in the local rates. In 1921, as a result of Britain's economic troubles, local authorities were told not to incur any new expenses; as one would expect, nursery provision was among the first schemes to be dropped. The socialist ideals of the new Labour government of 1929 were curtailed by the 1931 economic crisis, which resulted in the Board of Education refusing to sanction the building of new nursery schools, despite the government's view that they were 'comparatively inexpensive and an entirely efficient means of securing a fair start in life, even for infants whose home life is depressed'.

The 1930s were characterized by public authorities losing touch with the new attitudes towards nursery provision. The authorities continued to view nurseries in nineteenth-century terms:

> The fundamental purpose of the nursery school or class is to reproduce the health conditions of the good nursery in a well managed home and thus provide an environment in which the health of the young child, physical, mental and moral, can be safeguarded.
>
> (Hadow Report, Part III 1933)

The Nursery Schools' Association, however, suggested that the increase in the number of small private nurseries tended to show that nursery schools met a need felt by all types of families (Blackstone 1971). The decline in the number of domestic servants as working-class women opted for more lucrative occupations meant that middle-class women were increasingly in need of some support in the care and education of their young children. A growing interest in child psychology, the concept of sequential mental growth, and the belief that, although one's child's intelligence was largely predetermined, a stimulating environment, such as those in Montessori schools, would be of benefit, all helped to develop the view that nursery schools were places of education.

Declining birth rates, which resulted in fewer siblings, and the shrinking of middle-class households (due to the decrease in the number of domestic servants) led to a belief that young children needed to look beyond the home in order to develop socially. Once again, nursery schools could help.

In the ten years after the First World War, there were only 26 nursery schools in England. In the next ten years the number had increased to 103 (of which 57 were voluntary and 46 local-authority and direct-grant schools). It is perhaps not too cynical to suggest that the upsurge of middle-class interest in nursery education may account for the relatively rapid increase in the number of nursery schools over the same period.

The child-care books of the 1920s and 1930s were heavily influenced by characters such as Watson and Truby King, who felt that children's lives should be regimented and lived according to a timetable. Furthermore, too much affection between parents and children was not to be encouraged. In this climate of opinion the concept of maternal deprivation had no place in considerations about nursery provision.

The Second World War

The mushrooming of nurseries during the Second World War, and the rise in the number of working married women with children, is well known history. The war nurseries were administered nationally by the Ministry of Health and at a local level by the Maternity and Child Welfare departments. They were a blend of day nursery and nursery school. The full-time nurseries, which were accessible only to children of mothers in full-time employment, reflected the needs of their clients in that they were open from 12 to 15 hours a day to accommodate the long factory shifts many women worked. They were not free; a fee of one shilling (5p) a day was charged, for which the child received food and free medical attention (this was before the introduction of the National Health Service). Part-time nurseries were open during school hours only; although in theory they were available to a broader range of children, in practice children whose mothers were employed – full- or part-time – received priority.

Not everyone felt that state-aided nurseries were the best solution to the problem of caring for under-fives whilst their mothers worked. The Ministry of Labour had suggested earlier in the war that a supervised system of voluntary child-minding would be very much in line with the wartime ideology of pulling together, and announced that 'self-help is often the best help' (perhaps adding under its breath 'and the cheapest'). This scheme was not well received by the TUC or by women's groups such as the Women's Co-operative Guild. These groups felt that the child-minding schemes smacked more of 'making do' and did not consider that this was an appropriate attitude to have towards child care (Blackstone 1971).

At the peak of the war, around 1944, there were almost fifteen times as many nurseries with almost ten times as many children in them as in 1939. The prime motivation behind the provision of nursery facilities at this time is evident in the Ministry of Labour's close involvement in the decision-making surrounding the establishment of war nurseries. Factors the Ministry took into account included an assessment of the urgency of the demand for female labour in the area concerned and an analysis of how effective nursery provision would be in ensuring that more married women would work. The link in the policy-makers' minds between nursery provision and female labour was to prove long-lasting. In later decades it led to a blinkered approach, not only to the needs of working women, but also to the needs of mothers who chose to stay at home and, of course, to the needs of young children.

The Post-War Era

It has frequently been argued that after the Second World War women were squeezed out of paid employment and forced back into the home. The government, it is said, drastically cut pre-school provision and then later utilized the work of psychoanalysts such as Bowlby to justify its actions.

There is some truth in this analysis, but it fails to take into account the complexities of the period. Many women did indeed return to their homes. Nevertheless, although some did so because they felt that the jobs should be 'for the men', and some undoubtedly were compelled to do so by insufficient child-care facilities, many women probably gave up work after having made rational decisions based on their knowledge of the realities of female employment – e.g. low wages, long journeys, tedious jobs and long shifts. Another influencing factor was whether or not any particular area had a tradition of female employment; in areas with no such tradition women were less likely to work after the war. The policy-makers' attitudes, however, were heavily influenced by the expectation that women and children were naturally going to be at home.

The 1944 Education Act provided a ray of hope for the supporters of nursery provision. It empowered local authorities to provide for the education of children aged between 3 and 5, but stopped short of making it compulsory. The Ministry of Health, by contrast, seemed determined to ensure that the nursery system built up during the war was not going to be allowed to provide the foundation for further developments. In April 1946 the grant to local authorities for nursery provision was halved, with drastic results. Once nurseries had to compete with other services for a share of the rates it became apparent that they were low on the scale of priorities.

Women did not always take this cut in services passively. A group of women in Pudsey made national headlines when they decided to fight the local council's decision to close a day nursery. 'Wives seize a nursery,' the *Daily Express* reported in June 1946:

> Mothers locked themselves in the day nursery in Littlemore Road, Pudsey, this weekend and refused to open the doors until the police came in through the windows. It was protest no. 1 at Pudsey Council's decision to close the nursery because it was too expensive. Protest no. 2 will be a silent one. Thirty mothers will not turn up for work at local factories. . . . 'We have to stay at home to look after the children,' they say.

Here, women were utilizing their power as workers in a priority industry (textiles) to protest and fight for services of especial importance to themselves and their children.

A few local councils, notably the London County Council, put forward schemes for the expansion of nursery provision in 1947. But the nation's economic difficulties resulted in a cut in government spending on social services and so prevented any such schemes getting off the ground.

Rather than wanting all women to return to their homes, the government was in the position of desperately requiring women's labour in certain industries that would help Britain's sluggish economy. Nursery provision was seen as a means of luring women to work. Parliamentary debates reveal that many individuals were not convinced of the value of nursery education; yet, when the needs of young children were balanced against the needs of the economy, the economy won:

> In normal times, the proper place for young children is in the home, and however good a day nursery may be, it cannot equal a good home environment. But times are not normal . . . it is quite useless the government appealing to mothers to go to work unless they make provision for looking after the children.
>
> (Hansard 12 June 1947)

Day nurseries were, to the MP quoted here, obviously second best. None the less, in order to end clothes rationing and improve textile exports, he was willing for the nation's under-fives to receive second-best care.

A year later MP Barbara Castle was to highlight the link between an increased commitment to nursery provision and an increased desire for women's labour:

> It was not that there was no need in the Lancashire area for properly equipped and properly run day nurseries before the war – there was that need – but there was a different situation then because labour was abundant and employers were under no obligation to try to create inducements for women to go back to industry. They were able to rest in the assurance that women would come back to the industry because they would be driven to do so by the unemploy-ment of their men.
>
> (Hansard 28 May 1948)

This attitude towards pre-school provision has proved iniquitous. So long as a commitment to providing facilities for under-fives has been dependent upon the policy-makers' desire to attract women to join the work-force, the provision has been piecemeal, inadequate, not universally accessible and of a lower standard than those nursery facilities provided in recognition of the needs of pre-school children.

The spectre of maternal deprivation

The post-war years were characterized by an atmosphere of pro-natalism and concern for the family. Worries over the falling birth rate led to a number of measures designed to ease family life, e.g. family allowances. Within this framework of pro-natalism, nurseries and nursery centres were advocated but only as they 'freed' the mother, freed her to have more children (Riley 1979). John Bowlby's theories on the damaging effects of maternal deprivation (1952) gained currency during this period, and not only because the theories suited government policy.

The war had resulted in a number of changes. Communities had been physically shattered by the bombings and never fully recovered; families moved into new housing, which had not been planned with the mother and young child in mind. There was little opportunity for adults to socialize or for children to play in safe, communal areas. Mothers became increasingly isolated. Middle-class families who prior to the war had managed to retain domestic help suddenly found themselves having to cope alone. Inexperienced mothers had few people to turn to for advice or reassurance. Not only were Bowlby's views persuasively presented; they also seemed simple. So long as a mother stayed with her child, everything would be fine. Bowlby's assertion that 'mother-love in infancy and in childhood is as important for mental health as are vitamins and protein for physical health' (1953) encapsulated the view that mothers played an important role in the growth of their children into healthy and happy adults. The process by which motherhood was idealized during this period has been discussed in detail elsewhere (see for example Dally 1982); pro-natalism and Bowlbyism were important influences in the process.

In the 1950s the spread of such views helped dampen demands for nursery provision. Mothers would get their dose of Bowlbyism from a range of sources; the media, the women's magazines and the health visitors, who tended to pass on the wisdom of the day.

Much of what Bowlby said was misrepresented or misinterpreted. The more sensitive treatment of children in hospitals and in care undoubtedly owes much to Bowlby's theories, but assertions such as that full-time employment of the mother 'must be regarded as a potential source of deprived children'. (Bowlby 1952) were emotive and guilt-inducing. In (the same) vein, he stated that mothers of young children 'should not be free to earn' (Bowlby 1952), thus arguing for an increased family allowance whilst children were young. Whether Bowlby felt that this would reduce the economic pressures on families, which would therefore result in women not wanting to work, is not clear.

Such comments nevertheless suggest that, like many of his contemporaries, he believed that women worked only because of the money involved – a view that later surveys would perpetuate by, for example, the phraseology of the questions (Oakley 1981).

Bowlby's differential treatment of mothers and fathers is also interesting. 'Husbandless' mothers were to be given economic assistance to ensure they were able to stay at home and care for their children until the children were of an age 'to adapt to nursery schools'. 'Wifeless' fathers, however, were to be provided with a housekeeper service. The implication was that the 'mother love' so essential to young children was a female trait, and an employed house-keeper was more likely to be able to provide it than the child's own father.

Other child-care specialists such as Winnicott (1967) and Spock (1958) similarly emphasized the importance of the mother in the child's early years. The assumption that all women would find life at home with a young baby stimulat-ing, exciting and fulfilling runs through most of the child-care manuals of the time. No reference is made to women who did not find this to be so or to those living in less than ideal conditions.

> Talk about women not wanting to be housewives seems to ignore one thing, that nowhere else but in her own home is a woman in such command.
>
> (Winnicott 1967)

Nowadays such a comment would not necessarily be taken as an endorsement of the pleasures of home life.

Bowlby's theories not only affected how women felt about leaving their young children and pursuing their own interests, but also had an impact on nursery provision. His views provide a ready-made justification for the paucity of pre-school provision, especially for under-threes, and also facilitated the introduction of part-time nurseries in the late 1950s and 1960s. Many nurseries, being open during school hours only, were effectively part-time provision for mothers in full-time employment; but mothers' problems increased greatly when children began to attend nurseries for only half-day sessions. A prime motivation for the introduction of part-time provision was economic, since twice the number of children could receive nursery education for the same cost to the government as before. This reason was hardly likely to be popular, however. Instead the new organization was presented using more palatable and child-orientated justifications, by reference to Bowlby's view that even after the age of three mother–child separations should not be for too long a period.

The effect of Bowlbyism on the consciences of many women who had to go out to work – either to provide for their family or to maintain their mental health – goes unrecorded. Such theories of maternal deprivation ignore completely the many culturally diverse forms of child care, from the close-knit working-class communities that eixsted in many parts of Britain to the kibbutzim, collectives and extended families of other regions of the world. It is after all very recently that families in England itself have become nuclear and that women have been expected to devote themselves solely to their children without any respite for either mother or child.

Later developments

The pattern of state-aided nursery provision in the 1950s was much influenced by the view that a woman should not be working if she had young children. If she had to work, provision might be available but not guaranteed. If day care was required only because of the 'mother's desire to supplement the family income by going out to work', then the Ministry of Health declared that the cost should not be incurred by the state (1951). Nine years later, despite a growing demand for nursery provision, the government pulled the rug out from under the toddlers' feet yet again. It stated that not only had it been impossible in sixteen years to carry out the expansion referred to in 1944, but in addition it had no intention of doing so in the foreseeable future:

> No resources can at present be spared for the expansion of nursery education, and, in particular, no teachers can be spared who might otherwise work with children of compulsory school age.
>
> (Ministry of Education 1960)

In the 1950s and 1960s there was an increase in the number of children whose mothers worked. Also during this period the British government was engaged in an extensive recruitment drive for workers from abroad. The jobs on offer were generally of low status and poorly paid, often involving unsocial working hours. Parents who came to work as nurses or on public transport found that no thought had been given to the needs of workers such as themselves for flexible child-care facilities.

Working part-time did not necessarily solve the problem of child care, as a survey of mothers in the mid-1960s showed (Hunt 1968). This survey revealed that the overwhelming majority of mothers expressed a desire for preschool facilities, even for the under-twos. The women were critical of existing provision on the grounds that it was too expensive, too far away, the hours did not suit working parents and the facilities were over-subscribed. Eleven years later the situation had not improved much:

> 'These [council] nurseries are not for working mothers. It is difficult to get part-time work – at least until 12 o'clock. I could only get work with hours from 7.30 a.m. to 1.30 p.m. Too early to take my daughter to nursery and too late to collect her.'
>
> (CRC 1976)

The problems were greater for ethnic-minority than for white families. Even as late as the 1970s, when there was an apparent increased official interest in racism, a survey reported that, whilst over half the white children in the study were at nursery, only 17 per cent of black children and 7 per cent of Asian children were (CRC 1975). The researchers also suggested that access to pre-school facilities such as day nurseries probably depended on 'persistence, making a case and being visible to the local authority' (CRC 1975). Unfamiliarity with the system and language were great disadvantages.

In previous decades, as now, children from ethnic-minority groups faced racism not only in terms of gaining access to nursery facilities. Once the child had gained a coveted nursery place, the racism that is a feature of most institutions – including nursery schools, classes and day nurseries – began to operate. Parents were in a weak position. Did they complain or take their child away and begin the search for pre-school care all over again?

Audrey Hunt's survey in 1965 had little effect on policy. When confronted with the evidence that mothers wanted more day-nursery places, the Ministry of Health remained unmoved, saying airily:

> They have been provided by the Local Health Authorities since 1945 to meet the needs of certain children for day care on health and welfare grounds. This service is not intended to meet a demand from working mothers generally for subsidized day care facilities. The number of places provided is therefore considerably less than the demand shown.
>
> (Hunt 1968)

If women are supposed to be the experts in child care, it is odd that their opinions are given such scant regard.

Alternatives to state provision

Because of the inadequacy of state-aided provision, after the war women increasingly turned to child-minders and voluntary nursery provision. In 1967 Joan Lester MP told the House of Commons that it was about time the country made up its mind about working mothers: 'It is no use encouraging mothers of young children to go back to work or putting them in the economic situation where they have to go to work and not provide facilities whereby they can get their young children minded' (Hansard 24 April 1967). Lester said that in 1965 there were around 4.5 million under-fives and yet there was space for only 21,000 of them in the 448 local-authority day nurseries. She also pointed out that almost eight times more children were in private nurseries in 1965 than there had been sixteen years earlier, and that similar increases had occurred in the number of children being cared for by child-minders.

While being aware of the problems of child-minding (see for example Jackson and Jackson 1973), governments still praised this form of child care, as it was a flexible arrangement and was the most likely source for a young child of the 'continuous care' espoused by Bowlby – although research has shown that continuity is not one of the strong points of the child-minding system (Mayall and Petrie 1983). The system was also cheap – to the Exchequer. This complacent attitude, added to the belief that what people do in their own homes is up to them, has resulted in general inertia as regards improving child-minding.

One aspect in particular that has tended to be glossed over is the experience of ethnic-minority families. Children from families in which English was not the home language fared worst in terms of child-minding. A survey carried out in 1977–8 found that at least 34 per cent of child-minders were averse to taking children who did not speak English and/or were of a different ethnic background to themselves (Mayall and Petrie 1983). A child whose home language is not English is caught in a double bind. If the mother can find an English-speaking child-minder who will take her child, there are problems. Not only can the mother and minder not easily exchange information, but the child and the minder obviously experience communication difficulties. In addition the child suffers in not having sufficient opportunity to develop and extend her or his home language. The 1975 CRC study found that if an ethnic-minority child was placed with a minder who shared her or his ethnic and linguistic background there was a different set of problems to contend with. This time they centred on the difficulties experienced by ethnic-minority child-minders

in gaining access to minder support services; in common
with their clients, such child-minders are also often
hampered by poor environmental conditions.

A prime example of the voluntary provision that developed in the 1960s and 1970s is the playgroup movement,
whose history has been well documented elsewhere.
(Blackstone 1971; Van der Eyken 1977). This is undoubtedly
a valuable pre-school facility, run by dedicated and concerned individuals; but the policy-makers, in showering
the movement with praise, appear to have failed to realize
that playgroups are essentially a middle-class resource.
Access to the types of skill required and the necessary
facilities tend to be concentrated in the middle classes. In
addition, the emphasis on parental involvement and half-
day sessions tends to exclude the working mother and her
child.

White women in full-time employment find it difficult to
make satisfactory arrangements for child care. This is not
only because of the inadequacies of the system but also
because employers are often not willing to give time off to
enable parents to 'settle in' children, to care for sick children
or to take on the administrators at the local council in order
to ensure they pay for a child-minder, for example. Women
from ethnic-minority groups find it even more difficult.
Ethnic-minority families tend to be concentrated in the
areas of poor housing and are over-represented in the lower
income groups; ethnic-minority women are likely to be in
lower-paid jobs, often working longer hours. The CRC
study in 1975 noted that

> ethnic minority mothers were less able to get access to the
> day care provision they most desired than were white
> mothers; they had less access to subsidized or free services
> (day and nursery schools); they had greater difficulty in
> finding child minders near their home and found that their
> choices in minder were restricted.

Men and the under-fives

Men have hardly featured in this chapter except as financiers and child-care 'experts'. This is not a reflection of the contribution that men should make to the care and education of the under-fives, but rather of the sexism that has existed and still exists in the whole area of under-fives care.

Just as with women, men's role in the family began to change radically in the early nineteenth century as they were increasingly employed away from home. Previous to this, parents and children lived, worked and grew together. There is evidence that it was not uncommon for men, especially working-class men, to take a share of child care and housework, especially if the wife was employed. This was not so in middle-class households probably because servants were used.

In Staffordshire, for example, in the second half of the nineteenth century 'it was no uncommon sight to see a man cleaning and sweeping, caring for the children or even putting them to bed, on the evenings when the women were engaged with the family washing'; similarly an Edwardian miner's wife said of her husband 'I've seen him bathe 'em, oh aye, when they [the children] were new. . . . He'd do the cooking perhaps – well he'd help with the cooking any road' (both cited in Thompson 1975). These men were not taking an *equal* share of child care and housework, however, and for men who felt that as chief bread-winner they deserved to be waited on hand and foot there were always social conventions to give support: 'It was illegal for a man ever to use needle and cotton in those days. . . . A boy wasn't supposed to bake, he wasn't supposed to wash up, he wasn't supposed to make beds' (Thompson 1977).

In the early part of the twentieth century social convention ensured that most men kept away from small children. Later in the century the 'advisers' and child-care specialists – most of whom, ironically, were men – helped perpetuate the situation. The behaviourist Watson, whose views held sway in the inter-war period, noted that quiet play before bed was a good time for fathers to spend with their children: 'it keeps the child used to male society. They have a chance to ply him with questions' (Hardyment 1984). In the 1950s Buxbaum emphasized the importance of the father in providing a 'masculine' role figure. She tells of a problem family in which the mother worked and the father stayed at home the terrible result was that the six-year-old son insisted on copying his father and engaged in 'feminine' pursuits such as cooking and cleaning (Buxbaum 1951).

Bowlby (1952) refers to the father but only to explode any ideas a father may have about his importance to the young child:

> in the young child's eyes father plays second fiddle and his value increases only as the child's vulnerability to deprivation decreases. . . . [However] as illegitimate children know, fathers have their uses even in infancy. Not only do they provide for their wives to devote themselves unrestrictedly to the care of the infant but . . . they support her [the mother] emotionally.

Winnicott (1967) was to echo this view. 'Father can help,' he admitted, although he could not join the magic circle that the mother 'can make with her arms, in the centre of which is the baby'. Nevertheless, fathers did not need to feel totally rejected, since Winnicott felt that their 'knowledge of the world' would enable them to choose suitable toys for their children – something the children's mother was obviously incapable of doing, sheltered as she was at home. Throughout the child-care literature of this period the assumption is that fathers will be away from home for the greater part of the day and that their use is limited to that of provider and protector.

This lack of involvement by men in the care and education of very young children has probably resulted in the poor status of child carers (both paid and unpaid) and also in the trivializing of the work involved in the care and education of under-fives. In addition, despite the rise in the number of 'single parents' – in practice the majority of single parents are women – men have been particularly insensitive to the difficulties single parents face, especially in terms of child care.

Conclusion

It is paradoxical that developmental psychologists, psychoanalysts and doctors have all stressed the unique importance of an individual's first five years, and yet British governments have consistently refused to recognize this through the provision of adequate finance and support to carers of young children. Although in the 1960s, as in earlier decades, nursery provision was vigorously supported when it served the purpose of enticing mothers back to work (this time teachers), generally the recent history of nursery provision is depressing. The 1972 White Paper seemed finally to be according pre-school provision the place it deserves, with its recommendations for expansion. However, reading between the lines it is evident that even this paper is middle-class in orientation; full-time provision in nursery schools is advocated, but school hours are unsuitable if parents work full-time or on shifts. Even so, had the aims of the White Paper been achieved it would have been a step in the right direction.

Due to sexist attitudes towards working mothers, the lack of encouragement (by policy-makers in both the private and public sectors) for men to truly share the responsibilities of child care, and the generally low priority under-fives have in the eyes of decision-makers, the development of pre-school provision has always suffered from being seen as an 'extra' that the state can afford to neglect. As a chief education officer said in 1975: 'We are having to jettison everything we can to keep the ship afloat. Unfortunately nursery programmes are one of the most jettisonable items' (Day 1975).

CHAPTER 3

A comparative review of contemporary pre-school provision

SUE DUXBURY

The development of pre-school provision in Britain has been influenced by long-held traditions of family and child-rearing patterns, by the pervasive belief that child care is primarily the responsibility of women and by the lack of objective evidence concerning long-term effects of various childhood experiences. In addition, such provision is non-compulsory and therefore tends to be seen as peripheral, relying heavily on voluntary and self-help initiatives. Care and education are polarized, creating a further disjunction in provision, which reflects a division in society's attitude not only to children, but also towards women, parents and workers in the economy. This chapter discusses the relationship between women's work opportunities and child care, examines British provision, comparing it to that of Europe and beyond, and thirdly, assesses the prospects for future development.

Women, work and child care

More women now go out to work in Britain than in any other peacetime period, a trend seen throughout Europe.

As many as 69 per cent of women aged 16 to 59 are engaged in economic activity, and more return after childbirth with a shorter break after each child (Martin and Roberts 1984). The greatest increase is in part-time work, which is partly a reflection of the lack of child-care facilities in Britain.

According to the 1981 census, 2.6 million women in Britain with dependent children were in paid employment, yet the greatest influence on a mother's return to work is the age of her youngest child and the availability of suitable child-care arrangements (Cunningham and Curry 1981, Martin and Roberts 1984). The group with the lowest proportion of women working outside the home is mothers of pre-school children, which is not the case in many other countries (Boucher 1982, Martin and Roberts 1984, Pichault 1984).

More women would work in Britain if domestic commitments did not prevent them, and most women seeking work do so out of economic necessity, as do most men (Chaney 1981). Depression amongst mothers of young children tied to the home is well documented (Brown and Harris 1978), and work undoubtedly provides social contact, wage-earning capacity and personal credibility. Yet convenience of hours is the overriding criterion for eventual choice of work for mothers and married women, so that domestic routines can continue.

As a result, many women return to a lower level of work than before childbirth; most opt for part-time work (Martin and Roberts 1984), which tends to offer the least pay and security, and is usually concentrated in the typically 'female' service occupations, which often parallel domestic activities (Martin and Roberts 1984). Women from ethnic-minority backgrounds are the most disadvantaged as they tend to be concentrated in the lowest-paid occupations and have the least choice of child care (Mayall and Petrie 1983).

Child care is thus crucial to women's employment in Britain. A high proportion of working women rely on partners, parents and other family, rather than on institutionalized care, which is often unavailable or inappropriate for many working women. Almost half the women in Martin and Roberts's 1984 study had to pay for child care; most were responsible for arranging care, having time off for children's illnesses or visits; and although 83 per cent felt their husbands could have time off, often with pay, few chose to do so.

The majority of women still did all or most of the housework (73 per cent), but more said their husbands helped with child care. Oakley (1976), however, stresses that women overstate the amount of 'help' men give in the house, and it rarely constitutes a true fifty-fifty share. Thus society's expectation of women to be primarily mothers, child-carers and domestic workers severely restricts women's chances of employment, leaving them in a subordinate position in relation to men within the home and the labour market.

Types of pre-school provision

An exhaustive comparison of child care in and beyond Europe is neither practicable nor feasible due to the lack in some cases of directly comparable information. Nevertheless a brief glimpse of some other countries' attitudes towards child care, women and work is illuminating.

In contrast to Britain – which has one of Western Europe's poorest records of child-care provision in the maintained sector, yet the best voluntary and self-help record (Bruner 1980) – most European countries are politically and professionally committed to the view that parents are entitled to flexible and affordable child care (Equality for Children 1984). Most socialist or communist societies of Central and Eastern Europe operate official state day-nursery programmes, locating child care within a unified social and political philosophy. A more detailed examination of the provision that exists in rural and urban societies follows, grouped into the three sectors: state, voluntary and private.

State Provision

In Britain state provision consists of nursery schools and classes providing predominantly part-time education during school hours for 3- to 5-year-olds. The service is free, supervised by local education authorities and staffed by local nursery teachers and nursery nurses. In contrast, social services' day nurseries focus on care, open from 8 a.m. to 6 p.m. most weekdays of the year and provide full- or part-time places for children from a few months to five years old. Fees are means-tested; staffing comprises nursing officers, nursery nurses and helpers, and admission is increasingly on a priority basis. A few authorities operate family or children's centres combining care and education with other pre-school services, jointly administered by the education and social services. Of Britain's 3 million under-fives, 22 per cent receive nursery education, a further 18 per cent are admitted to primary school at four years or more, and only 1 per cent attend council day nurseries (Equality for Children 1984).

In France the government provides full-time care for 33 per cent of 2-year-olds and 88 per cent of 3-year-olds; Iceland for 21 per cent of 2-year-olds; Denmark 29 per cent; with Britain hardly catering for this age group at all. There is only limited agreement in any country about the most desirable form of day care for young children, and only a limited basis for the comparison of statistics even where statistics exist. Studies (CERI Centre for Educational Research and Innovation 1977, Goutard 1980, Equal Opportunities Commission 1984) suggest problems regarding regional differences, estimates of supply and demand, and the lack of monitoring of carers' nationality. Most countries make a major distinction in provision, either by age (0 to 3, 3 to school age), e.g. Austria, France and the Netherlands, or by function (care or education), as in the UK. Only a few countries have a unitary system combining care and education with the co-operation of all relevant ministries (e.g. health, education, welfare and law), as in Denmark and the Federal Republic of Germany.

Types of provision vary throughout Europe, as in Britain.

Day nurseries are the most highly sought after but their overall provision is low. Even in countries where total provision is high (France and Belgium), child-minders compete with or exceed day-nursery provision (Pichault 1984). The size and quality of day nurseries vary enormously, from the largest in Greece with 65 places, to the smallest in Germany with 27 places, which in turn affects the quality of provision.

A few countries have adopted or are moving towards the concept of integrated pre-school services: Denmark, France, Sweden, Belgium and to a small degree Britain. Few countries operate 24-hour nurseries, with extended day nurseries being available for a small percentage of children in Belgium, France and Denmark.

The Soviet Union and Japan have developed collective upbringing since the 1950s. Japan's kindergarten provision has increased sevenfold since the late 1950s, and by 1970 over 50 per cent of primary-school pupils had attended one. Significantly, less than half are maintained by the government, and overall provision still lags behind that in France, Britain and the USA. Day nurseries provide for 22 per cent of 0- to 5-year-olds, operating a similar curriculum to the kindergartens (Kobayash 1976).

In socialist and communist countries children are brought up collectively, socialized and educated into acceptable forms of behaviour and achievement, and are valued highly as the nation's future resource. In the 1970s the Soviet Union, for example, provided for over 10 per cent of under-twos in public nurseries, and 20 per cent to 3- to 6-year-olds attended pre-school. Some boarding schools and schools of the prolonged day are available for children of parents who work on shift or away (Bronfenbrenner 1974).

China has also followed the collective child-care trend, but as yet school attendance is not compulsory at any age. Crèches are run by local groups and by people's councils in rural communes and urban factories, and the demand for pre-schooling exceeds supply in the cities (Price 1979). More 2+-year-olds are catered for than in the West,

enabling more parents to work. Crèches provide for
1+-year-olds, some for eight to ten hours a day, with a few
boarding places. Kindergartens provide for some 3- to 7-
year-olds, under the Ministry of Education, where children
engage in twenty minutes' production daily and also grow
their own vegetables. Priority is given to children of
peasants, soldiers and workers, and success depends on
the wealth of the area and the teachers' expertise. Conditions tend to be spartan and apparatus minimal; the
status and pay of teachers (who often suffer from mental
illness due to the heavy work-load) are low (Manger *et al.*
1974).

Yugoslavia is moving towards an integrated pre-school
policy that reinforces the collective comradeship of children
and gives equal rights and services to all parents, thus
removing the burden of choice between work or child care.
Yugoslavia's national policy is committed to children, and,
as in other socialist countries, child abuse and molesting are
apparently almost unknown, with few children being
admitted to local-authority care. No distinction is made
between care and education, and it is accepted that most
women will work outside the home. At present Yugoslav
schools are overcrowded, staff ratios too high and the level
of care often unsatisfactory. Parents would like more involvement, as they believe happens in the West, but there
is no patronizing or tension between parents and professional carers, which is common in the West. The
programme is backed by a much more generous slice of
national resources than Britain allocates its pre-school
children (Penn 1984).

In some countries more state-aided child-care provision
is becoming necessary, as increasing numbers of rural
workers are being drawn to the cities. In India attempts
have recently been made to provide mobile crèches for the
children of migrant workers in Bombay and the larger
cities. In the last nine years more than 16,000 children have
been catered for in 108 centres, which aim to provide basic
care and education. This system now extends to other
children from 0 to 12 years, six days per week, funded by

international and government aid (National Childcare Campaign 1984).

In the Middle East attempts are being made to counteract the problems of living in occupied territories under patriarchal rule in which women are defined as child-carers and servants. In Palestine the women's movement is gaining ground in cities and refugee camps, and day care is seen as crucial to free women to leave the home, attend basic skills classes to get a job, and develop their health, education and self-reliance.

Egypt can not yet afford good schools for the young, who often have to share a building in three shifts. Informal programmes are needed but are regarded as too costly, but with the increase of women working the Ministry of Social Affairs is making attempts to meet the need for child-care and to control minding agencies. Some nursery homes and schools are developing in cities, and it is hoped this will spread to rural areas. The country is still in need of nursery personnel, the co-operation of executive bodies and the research to ascertain the needs of pre-school children (Hyde 1978).

Voluntary Provision
In Britain the highest proportion of provision is met by the voluntary and private sectors. Development has been of an *ad hoc* nature; governments tend to underplay their significance, and accurate statistics are not easily available. The voluntary sector provides playgroups, mainly under the auspices of the Pre-school Playgroups Association, which began as an initiative by middle-class parents to compensate for the lack of nursery schooling. About 80 per cent of playgroups currently belong to the PPA, catering for more than half a million children per year (Bruner 1980). They receive some local-authority grants, charge nominal fees and encourage parental involvement. Sessions are part-time once or more per week for children aged 2½ to 5 years. Staff are PPA-trained organizers or volunteer helpers, usually mothers. Other forms of playgroups run along similar lines are funded by charitable organizations,

e.g. Dr Barnardo's or Save the Children, often catering for a specific need, such as the care of mentally or physically disabled children.

A new development in the last five to ten years has been the small growth of community nurseries (about 50 to 100 in number), usually funded by urban aid or inner-city programmes. These aim to provide day care within the community, involving parents at policy, administration and care levels. Some charge is made, but the intention is to provide accessible, flexible day care for all local children whose parents require it.

Britain remains the leader in the field of self-help initiatives, which are almost incomprehensible to some European visitors. Only a few European countries operate such provision. Belgium has some joint or self-managed nurseries (e.g. in universities) and playgroups run by networks of women who work part-time, a system also found in Luxembourg. France has some alternative day nurseries run by parental associations with closer involvement and access to state schools.

In many pre-industrial societies, children are an integral part of the community and learn by experiencing the environment, acquiring skills and accepting responsibilities at first hand. In rural Africa, South America and China young children are often left in charge of domestic animals, and in the West Indies girls of six or seven are left to look after younger siblings when parents go to work (Comer 1974). In Britain, by comparison, children are often discouraged from attempting adult activities and denied responsibility; their true potential is often underestimated (Thompson 1972, in Comer 1974).

In close-knit societies, particularly rural ones, where there is a well-developed family network, the care of young children is seen as a shared family responsibility. In Matabeleland, for example, the eldest sister of the family becomes responsible for her own children and those of her daughters and younger siblings. Little distinction is made between the biological mother and other female relatives, and it is regarded as unnatural for a woman to show more interest in her own children than in others (Boulton 1983).

In many parts of rural Africa it is still common to find young children involved in the social and working life of the family. Babies are equally integrated, observing the whole family at work from the secure position of the caretaker's back. This caretaker could be an older sibling or another adult relative. It has been shown that children and babies gain considerably from such experiences:

> by living and working in cooperation with adults, children in traditional African society thus receive the developmental experiences which their Western counterparts, because of their exclusion from adult society, have to acquire through the specially constructed environment of the nursery school . . . the precocious early development of rural African infants is not found among the babies of the urban elite.
>
> (Gender Rules OK 1979)

Child-Minders and Private Provision

Bridging the private and voluntary sectors are child-minders – individuals, usually women, who care for other people's children in their own home. In Britain by law they should be registered with the local social services department, which may offer support, equipment and training. In 1980, 99,000 under-fives were cared for by 39,500 registered minders (Pichault 1984), but an estimated 150,000 were cared for by unregistered minders, who vary considerably in cost and the quality of provision (CERI 1977). The quota for child-minders varies throughout Europe, from the lowest of 1.5 children per minder in France to a staggering 16 per minder in Greece.

Child-minding generates as much debate in Europe as in Britain yet it remains the most utilized if not the most preferred form of child care. In some countries the role of the minder is clear; she is registered and protected by laws defining function, status and pay, as in France where minders receive benefits, unemployment pay and paid holidays. In Denmark family day-carers are government sponsored and unionized, and have a contract, supervision and support. A suggested European charter for child-minders was met with an unenthusiastic reception (except by Greece) as being too impractical (see Pichault 1984).

In Britain an increasing number of children are being cared for in the private sector, in private nurseries – 19,900 in 1980 (Pichault 1984) – or by nannies, au pairs or mothers' helps in the child's own home, particularly among pro-fessional women and more affluent families (Mackie 1985). The conditions and pay for such carers rarely reflect the responsibility and demands of the job. Criticisms from the women's movement also suggest that professional women are gaining their independence by exploiting other women (Mackie 1985).

A very few employers provide workplace nurseries offer-ing day care whilst employee parents, usually mothers, work on-site; 72 nurseries catered for 2,100 children in 1980 (Pichault 1984). A charge is usually made, the age catered for and standard of provision vary, and registration is terminated with leaving the employment. Many workplace nurseries are under threat of closure, and employers have little incentive to open nurseries when female labour is abundant (Moss 1978, Mottershead 1978).

General trends in pre-school provision

Funding
The general trend throughout Europe is one of cutting back or increasing only in line with inflation. Only Denmark, Greece, Italy and the Netherlands plan to increase public spending to meet rising costs (and Denmark has to contain expenditure for the late 1980s because of the burden on national resources). Greece is only keeping up with rising costs, and Italy's plans for nursery expansion have been dropped, maintaining only the 1977 level (Pichault 1984). No country in the EEC grants day-care costs at a national level, although Greece and France do in certain regions, and Britain for a very small percentage of special cases. In

France and Luxembourg day-care costs are deductible expenses for tax purposes. Overall the expenditure on pre-school education remains low, with Britain one of the least generous countries (CEC, Commission of the European Communities 1981).

Goutard (1979) concludes that some problems in nursery provision are common throughout Europe including job losses (Belgium), attaining part-time status (Luxembourg), long hours and lack of relief staff (Netherlands). In Britain nursery teachers have little opportunity for promotion, no career structure and a lack of status despite apparent equality (NAS/UWT 1978). This is not the case in Denmark, one of the few countries with a career ladder for pre-school workers, who may train as a minder, progress to be a nursery teacher and with additional training become a centre leader or lecturer or move into the fields of child welfare, education or psychology. The lack of career opportunities may account for the fact that very few men are involved in nursery provision. Goutard (1979), however, suggests that despite the encouragement to train men, few stay very long; most transfer to other age ranges or quickly become advisers or inspectors.

Supply and Demand

The supply of pre-schooling falls short of demand in all EEC countries to differing degrees; in many, both have increased, leaving the gap unchanged (CERI 1977). Financial restraint is common to all governments but they may choose to withhold or release funds to pre-school provision and make individual interpretations of society's role, emphasizing the state, parents or both. In the CERI study of nine countries in and beyond Europe, none were satisfied with both quality and quantity of provision. France, one of the highest providers, was concerned about its quality and poor staff ratios – 1 to 40 in *écoles maternelles* for 2- to 5-year-olds. Sweden desired more specialist trained nursery teachers, and the Netherlands reported a disparity in quality and quantity of provision, depending on age levels 0 to 4 or 3 to 6. Levels of provision must also be considered in relation to the compulsory school age, which on average in Europe is 6, with Scandinavians starting at 7 and Britons at 5 (Pichault 1984).

The demand for day care has increased for under-threes in Europe in the last twenty years (currently a stable population of 10 million under-threes), accompanied by an increased economic activity rate of women. This has resulted in the problem of child care overriding all others where both parents or the only parent works outside the home, often resulting in a great disparity between real preference and eventual choice of care (Martin and Roberts 1984, Pichault 1984). Despite the CEC recommendation to all member states that all children irrespective of social class be given the opportunity to attend a pre-school establishment by the age of three at the latest (CEC 1979), innovation for day care for under-threes has not moved observably forward.

There are only just over a million children under three catered for by services in the EEC, and two-thirds of these places are in France (Pichault 1984). As provision for over-threes is just beginning to gain acceptance, that for under-threes continues to be hampered by conflicting child-care philosophies, by the lack of a unified policy and by fragmented action, all too familiar to providers of over-threes services, which remain inadequate for many working parents.

Employment Practices
The expansion and improvement in child-care provision must be accompanied by changes in employment practices and conditions if women are to assume equality in the workplace and men are to take a fair share of domestic responsibility. Measures are necessary, firstly, to enable parents to meet child-care requirements, e.g. settling a child at nursery/carers, time to care for sick children or to visit children's services (Pogrebin 1982).

Secondly, to afford parents choice in allocating time between employment and family there needs to be an increase in flexible working hours, as in Switzerland and

West Germany (OECD 1977). Increased opportunities for part-time work at all levels are necessary in all types of occupation (with the same pay, conditions and security as full-time work). Parents of dependent children should have the right to part-time work at a comparative level, a minimum paternity leave and longer-term leave for both parents with compensation for loss of earnings, as available in Sweden by extended National Insurance.[1]

Recent submissions by the Equal Opportunities Commission (EOC 1984b, 1985) to the House of Lords and Department of Employment, on proposals for a directive on parental leave and leave for family reasons, met a mixed reception. The Lords Select Committee concluded that there should be EEC legislation to provide for parental leave in order to promote equality of opportunity for women and improve child care, and would therefore support a draft directive on these grounds. The committee found no positive or negative evidence to suggest that parental leave would raise industry's costs; but due to the important social objectives, any increased costs should be met by governments. Small businesses of less than twenty workers would be exempt. Subject to the EEC minimum of one month's leave, each member state should decide the length of leave with benefits payable in a manner decided by each state – preferably from public funds.

On the question of leave for family reasons, the Lords committee felt that legislation *should not* and *could not* provide for such leave, and that the directive should be amended accordingly, after which it would recommend it to the House for debate.

The Department of Employment (EOC 1985) was decidedly less enthusiastic about both types of leave. It stressed that the government stongly believes such matters are best determined voluntarily between employers and employees on a priority/need/circumstances basis.

The EOC, in disagreement, stresses that the absence and exclusion of fathers from statutory provision of leave for childbirth and child care leads to an assumption these are only 'women's concerns', thus discriminating simultaneously against women and men. The costs must be weighed against the advantages of retaining skilled staff after parental leave and a reduction in unemployment payments.

At present seven EEC countries have some form of parental leave either established or in government proposals. Only two have leave available only to mothers (EOC 1985).

Available Child Care for Working Parents
In many parts of Europe changes in family structure have resulted in fewer available relatives for child care and a subsequent increase in the use of child-minders. Yet in 1981 only 3 per cent of child-minder users preferred that type of care (Cunningham and Curry 1981). This trend was also noted by Pichault (1984) throughout Europe, except in Denmark and Sweden where minders are well trained, monitored and supported. More affluent women may be able to afford nannies or live-in help – most commonly used in Denmark, Iceland and Germany (Pichault 1984) – but as Mackie (1985) points out, in Britain their pay is low, status ambivalent and work-load high.

Local-authority day nurseries are catering for fewer children of working families. Intake is on priority basis (e.g. physically or emotionally at risk children), and waiting lists are excessively long. It is particularly difficult to find child care for children with special needs whose parents wish to work.[2]

Workplace nurseries are few and far between. Only 25,000 all-day factory kindergarten places existed in 1976 (Moss 1978). These often reflect employers' rather than employees' needs, assume that child care is a problem only of female employees and may be withdrawn if unprofitable.

Private nurseries, flourishing more in the South than in the North of Britain, may vary in cost and quality of provision but would be beyond the scope of many poorer working women. Nursery schools and classes and also playgroups were not intended for working parents, although a few extended day projects in both areas have begun but tend to be focused in Inner London.

Other voluntary initiatives rarely cater for the full range of parents' working hours and require a high degree of parental involvement. This has been discussed more fully by Janet Finch (1984a and 1984b), and further consideration of this work appears in Chapter 6. Both state and voluntary provision, usually based upon rigid hours, tends even where available to be inappropriate for working parents (Moss 1978).

The problem of child care for working parents in Britain is exacerbated by the perceived division between care and education, whereas an appropriate provision should offer both (Mottershead 1978). The lack of provision for under-twos also reflects the view that young children should be at home with their mother (Leach 1979); yet many other countries accept that women do work and provide child care accordingly – although few in sufficient quantity and quality.

The demand is clear, yet it requires long protracted effort to translate it into provision, and even longer to affect the way decisions regarding the balance between employment and child care are made. Job flexibility and appropriate child-care provision are both necessary before individuals can make realistic choices. The current *ad hoc* approach is inadequate to meet the demand for a comprehensive service. Successive governments have been unwilling to assume responsibility for the children of working parents and those below school age.

Moss (1978) calls for direct state and state-aided provision with a declining reliance on workplace or private service. He believes that voluntary bodies should have more finan-cial and professional support and that governments must take a more active role in planning and co-ordinating expansion, as in Sweden. Tension between various types of staff could be reduced in a fully integrated system with co-ordinated training and a career structure as in Denmark (EOC 1978). Total responsibility should come under one department, unified at central government level, breaking down barriers between care and education.

The future

The outlook for the future of British pre-school provision is not bright. There are no plans to increase day-nursery provision; rather, its range of customers is contracting (Penn 1984), unlike in many countries where every child is regarded as an equal priority. Despite the plans to develop nursery education after Plowden, the 1980 Education Act absolved local education authorities of the obligation to provide it, leaving it a discretionary matter. Proposals to extend nursery school hours arouse debates as to whether the children of working parents would be segregated or whether staffing problems could be overcome. Only three British education authorities currently operate such a service, compared to France's coverage for 85 per cent of 3- to 5-year-olds and 23 per cent of 2-year-olds.

In contrast to many European countries, which are fighting to maintain and improve pre-school provision, Britain lost 1,000 nursery places in 1982, and many more will go with lower rate-support grants (Bayliss 1985). The areas with the highest levels of pre-school provision, and also the highest level of deprivation, will face the severest penalties.

Rate-capping will also affect the voluntary/aided sector (an area of provision not considered necessary in many European countries because of their levels of state provision). Playgroups and charitable and urban organizations will cease to function if aid is withheld, leaving an ever-increasing gap in provision. Child-minders, instead of being supported within an integrated system, as in Denmark, will have their role diminished with cuts in the authority support that provides equipment and group facilities.

The under-fives, highly valued in many societies as the future resource, are in Britain under the greatest threat because their provision is non-statutory and accorded low priority. The government reaffirms by these drastic actions the belief that child care is the responsibility of the family, namely the mother (Hughill 1984). Both historical and cross-cultural perspectives suggest, however, that attributing responsibility for child care to the biological mother, whose primary duty is held to be domestic, is a peculiarity of Western industrialized societies and is not the 'natural common sense' it is made out to be. This way of thinking denies women the right to work and men the right to share in their home and children, which many other countries are attempting to ensure.

Notes

1. Despite the apparent equality in Sweden, however, Pogrebin (1982) warns that it is still not Utopia. Women tend to be concentrated in the less prestigious jobs. In most two-career couples the woman still does most of the housework, and despite the availability of paternal leave only 12 per cent of men take the six weeks after childbirth and only one-third care for a sick child.
2. Fewer places for children of one-parent families are available despite the Finer Report's conclusion that they have a special need to work (Frost 1981). Further, despite the Warnock Report's recommendation to provide for and integrate disabled children into pre-school provision, such arrangements remain limited.

CHAPTER 4

The beginnings of sex stereotyping

PAULINE FRANCE

When Kiran, my son, was approaching his second year we started going to a co-operatively run nursery, where he could play with children older and younger than himself. Parents at this nursery take an active role in organizing and participating in children's play. One day Kiran and a few other children were playing outside. Kiran's pleasure in his developing running skills became apparent, as he ran about shouting with delight. A., the mother of a 2½-year-old girl, commented in an approving tone, 'Oh, he's a real boy. So full of energy.' I agreed that he did have energy, but added that many girls can be just as energetic. I then talked about the calm activities, like sharing stories and painting, that Kiran also enjoyed.

A little later A.'s daughter joined Kiran but was quickly warned not to mess up her 'pretty canvas sandals'. Then the girl initiated a new game: kicking a large ball for Kiran to return. Both children enjoyed this collaborative activity so much that they started shouting. Immediately the girl was told to be quiet by her mother, because 'ladies don't shout and make a noise like that'. My very tentative protests that both children were enjoying themselves and that the girl was a skilful ball-kicker did not serve to keep the play going.

This incident highlights the way sex role and behaviour difference are established in the daily lives of very young children. At the time I faced a series of questions and conflicting interests that could be resolved only through regular contact with A. over a period of months:

(1) Firstly I was in a situation where mainly women come with their children in a spirit of equality and co-operation. The talk between adults can be stimulating, friendly, sociable and very supportive. Women have an identity beyond being so-and-so's mother. Naturally I did not want to sour my relationship with any of the women in this setting by challenging ideas in a way that seemed antagonistic. I was aware that, like all of us, A. was trying to raise her child in a patriarchal society, where women and girls are held in check. In-depth discussions are also not practical in a busy nursery.

(2) I felt that A.'s comments about Kiran's and her daughter's behaviour needed to be balanced by an alternative viewpoint in front of the children. She was giving voice to a commonplace view: that boys and girls are different and should behave so. This notion can have a limiting effect on both boys and girls by reducing or diverting their options. For a boy to be a 'real boy' he must look and act the part – running, shouting, taking the lead, not caring about appearance or showing any signs of 'weakness'. For a girl to 'act like a lady' she must be the exact opposite – quiet, passive, dependent and careful about her appearance (Browne and France 1985).

(3) I was unsure whether A. intended to stop both children shouting, which is what happened, or whether she honestly believed it was acceptable for a boy to be noisy. I took the fact that she had already approved of Kiran shouting to be a confirmation that she was reinforcing sex-differentiated behaviour.

(4) The way the girl had been dressed meant that she would find it hard to enjoy all the facilities of the nursery. Her open-toed sandals were inappropriate for climbing and might easily be splashed if she engaged in painting or

water-and-sand play. She was already learning, like many other girls have and will, that dressing 'prettily' can get in the way of activity and exploration. Girls have to make choices: engage only in activities that suit 'pretty' clothes or attempt to wear more appropriate clothes – a hard choice for any two-year-old.

Why do incidents like this happen all too often in children's lives? What can anti-sexist parents and teachers do to broaden children's experiences and avoid channelling children into narrowly defined and unequal sex roles? The following sections tackle these questions: firstly, by giving an overview of the various influential theories that tend to describe and explain sex differences; then by considering how a patriarchal society like Britain's is upheld from generation to generation, drawing on my experience as a parent and teacher in London; thirdly, by suggesting some strategies that may help our children grow up with an approach to life that does not rely on sex and race stereotypes.

What the 'experts' say

Many scientific theories that have attempted to demonstrate and explain differences between people, or between groups of people, have been built on the 'nature/nurture' debate, i.e. on a discussion of whether differences can be accounted for in terms of heredity or environment. John Archer points out that an adherence to one or other viewpoint has implications for any attempts at change or the development of appropriate social policy:

> For example if one takes the view that criminals are such because of their genetic make-up, the implication is that money spent on improving social conditions as a way of eradicating crime will be largely wasted. However, if one takes the view that some environmental conditions are the important factors, one can then suggest social remedies to prevent crime.
>
> (1978)

By analogy we can say that the biological explanation for sex-differentiated behaviour means that nothing can be done to change the status quo. An environmental approach allows for change within the growing child's social setting. The biological explanation of sex differences pivots on the assertion that women are intellectually inferior to men. It is believed that women alone possess from birth the personality traits and emotional characteristics that will suit them for their preordained role as carers, housekeepers and dependants. A growing body of research has shown up the flaws in such a theory, which is in reality an expression of the theorists' own biased opinion of women's capabilities and role in society (Archer 1978, Griffiths and Saraga 1979, Bland 1981).

The comprehensive research reviews of Maccoby and Jacklin (1974) and Fairweather (1976) have shown that the extent of proved differences between males and females has been greatly exaggerated. Much substantiated evidence for sex differences in human beings comes from studies of animal behaviour. Griffiths and Saraga (1979) point out that Corinne Hutt's (1972) conclusion that greater male achievement is due to males' greater persistence and single-mindedness is based on evidence from studies of chicks! They conclude that

> the dominant ideology of our society encourages us to believe that the social order is not only legitimate but also 'natural' and hence inevitable. Biologically based explanations of human social behaviour provide an important input into this ideology . . . but how can a biologically based explanation account for very rapid social change, such as the events of the Chinese revolution?
>
> (1979)

Given theoretical criticisms of biological explanations it is surprising to find so many people still continuing to promote such ideas. Possibly the support these theories give to current ideology helps to preserve them; also, they are much easier to understand than an analysis based on an amalgam of factors corresponding to the complex reality.

Western society is still experiencing the overwhelming influence of Freud's developmental psychology. Like many other feminists, Marielouise Janssen-Jurreit has criticized the patriarchal bias in his theoretical framework and shown that Freudian-orientated anthropologists and psycho-analysts have been responsible for perpetuating the idea of sex-differentiated behaviour (1982). Joan Bean has pointed out that Freud's theory of sex role development

> assumes the overriding significance of biology and early experience . . . [and] predicts a lifelong stability of masculine qualities for males and feminine qualities for females, ignoring the influences of the cultural environment.
>
> (1978)

Bean provides a critical review not only of Freud's model but also of two other theories that have been influential in the twentieth century. Both of these focus on the environmental factors that affect sex-role behaviour. The first is a social learning theory based on Skinner's learning theory of stimulus, response and reinforcement. Here the child is in the passive position of acquiring appropriate sex-role behaviour through a series of rewards and punishments from people in the environment. This theory denies any individual choice or the possibility of adopting an alternative sex role. The other theory considered by Bean does place the child in a more active role. This is the theory developed by Kohlberg from Piaget's cognitive stage framework. Kohlberg considers that a child learns sex-appropriate behaviour as a function of interaction with the immediate environment. Two-thirds of the children that he questioned could tell the sex of a doll shown to them by the time they reached forty months. He concluded:

> as soon as the boy categorises himself as being male he will value positively the objects and acts that agree with his gender identity.
>
> (1975)

It is revealing of Kohlberg's own attitudes that he has concentrated his research on the responses of boys.

Sex-identification theories like this have been amply

criticized by Selma Greenberg (1979). She shows that one implication of such theories is that boys are assumed to have nothing to learn from women; yet, in a society where women have the major responsibility for early child care, 'A boy is likely to be at home with one adult whom he has neither to walk like, talk like, think like or act like.' Girls, in being discouraged from identifying with their fathers, will be denied 'the world of knowledge, skills and opportunities that greater social access and preferential social treatment have given them [the fathers]' (Greenberg 1979). From my own experience of boys being raised principally by their fathers and thus seeing men in a caring role, it is still possible to find these boys behaving at times very differently from the male model they have.

A general criticism of all these theories of sex-role development, expressed by various writers (Archer 1978, Bean 1978, Rowan 1979), is that the status quo is upheld uncritically by such theorists. They come from and reinforce the ideology of sexism that permeates the society at all levels.

Alternative models of child development must challenge this rigid adherence to the concept of male and female as opposite sexes, and to the notion of clearly differentiated, unalterable sex roles. They must also take into account that each child is an individual actively involved in her or his development who will profit from being able to develop abilities, interests and personality as broadly as possible, without being restricted into narrow stereotypes. In addition a theory should recognize that there are as many differences between people of the same sex as there are between the sexes (Griffiths and Saraga 1979).

The preservation of differentiated sex roles is a highly political issue in a patriarchal society. The attributes traditionally assigned to men of being aggressive, competitive and dominating serve to bolster such a society, and violence becomes an important tool to keep 'women feeling fearful, inferior and inadequate so that they do not even contemplate revolt' (Rowan 1979). Although Rowan confirms that some male psychologists and sociologists, in addition to many feminists, have written about the value to society gained from the breakdown of patriarchy, the question still remains whether their perception has had any impact on child-raising theory and practice.

'Do what I say': patriarchy perpetuated?

Criticisms of traditional theories have hardly percolated into the lives of people involved in child care in Britain. A child is born into a society bound by rules and standards. These help to perpetuate the notion that there are sex differences. Underlying this idea are certain assumptions, which are transmitted through a range of influential sources. New parents become willing or unwitting upholders of the same values and sex-role stereotypes that have restricted their own horizons. Parents will be given advice from four main sources: the family network, professional advisers, the community (especially the peer group) and the media.

Family Network

Value judgements are expressed in homespun truths transmitted from one generation to the next. The authority structure within families, which rests on a sense of allegiances, makes it difficult for new parents to challenge, if they want, the sex-stereotyped views of their relatives. Older relatives may respond to a challenge by referring to their longer-standing experience as parents.

Professionals

Not only is there a ready-made network of advisers created by family and friends of new parents, but industrial society has also created a network of experts and professionals, from the areas of health, education and social services. They form an influential body of opinion, yet in many ways serve to bolster up the status quo, by presenting society as dominated by a white middle-class male élite. Challenging traditional views here can be even more precarious; these people are responsible for decisions that may affect your child's health, social welfare and educational future.

Community and Peer Group

The power of the community must not be underestimated. A new parent may be drawn into a closer relationship with people, including other parents, in the community and will feel considerable pressure to conform to the norms expressed in that environment. Anyone and everyone feels capable of offering advice and criticism about how to look after a child.

Power of the Media

The images of people's roles in society presented by the media are still clearly sex-differentiated. There have been challenges made, especially to advertisers, yet very little has changed. Women are still housewives, mothers and sex objects; men are still busy paid workers controlling the lives of others, being aggressive, adventurous and competitive (Matlow 1980, McRobbie and McCabe 1981).

The Four Assumptions

The major sources of influence on parents described above ultimately have an effect on their children, who also learn about society from their parents and their peers. Underlying the patriarchal outlook, and reflected in social policy and legislation, are the following assumptions, which uphold the notion of sex differences.

Assumption 1: women and men must adopt different roles from each other when they become parents.

If, like Lesley Holly (1982), we conduct a survey of the images of parents that are presented by the media and by magazines and booklets from professional organizations such as the British Medical Association, the Royal Society of Medicine and the Health Visitors' Association, we find that the ideology of motherhood, popularized by Bowlby and followers, is enjoying a resurgence. Leading child-care writers, such as Penelope Leach and Gordon Bourne, promote this image. Throughout, the parental model is of a white, heterosexual married couple, who demonstrate sex-differentiated characteristics and undertake different roles serving to maintain a male-dominated family structure.

To be a 'proper mother' a woman is expected to be a warm, loving carer, responsive to the physical and emotional needs of child and father. She must become unpaid 'housewife' as well as mother, married to all the domestic chores involved in running a home. Payment for such work is beyond discussion, yet no paid worker is expected to undertake all the cleaning, repairing and cooking that will happen in the workplace.

Whilst Holly has pointed out that a new image has been discovered by some social commentators, she considers that it is a token image and that it

> creates an illusion no more liberating than the last. . . . so men continue to enjoy their children and family life without having to give up social and economic power, or routinely be involved in the hard work of family life and child rearing.
>
> (1982)

David Piachaud's study into the time it takes mothers to care for their pre-school-aged children confirms Holly's view that it is a myth to claim fathers take a full and sometimes equal share in the care of their children. Piachaud found that mothers are responsible for nine out of every ten hours spent on 'life support tasks' (e.g. feeding, washing, nappy changing), whilst fathers take on only one in ten hours (1984).

A man is expected to subordinate any inclinations towards an active role in child-rearing to the demands of providing financially for 'his' family. In return he is acknowledged as head of the household (as assumed in a question still posed on the UK electoral registration form). He can get away with only a token nod at housework – often in the form of maintenance and repair, i.e. jobs that can be done by paid workers if no one in the household is able to take them on.

Within such a rigid framework men and women are both losers, especially in the early stages of raising a child.

Women are forced to give up or limit all hopes of a career or job outside the home and of developing their identity as people other than as mothers. Men miss an opportunity to develop the caring side of their character and to enjoy the stimulation (as well as the hard work) of raising a child and forming a close, influential relationship with that child. This sharp division of roles can create tensions between men and women, who become absorbed in their own areas of expertise and may find themselves in conflict where there are clashes of interest.

Women are often in the position of doing an elaborate balancing act with their time to embark on a wage-earning job, in addition to their role as mother and housekeeper. This hard-earned contribution to the family income is rarely given enough credit. For economic reasons many women are forced into employment where they may be exploited and given little control (e.g. in trade union activity).

In my own recent experience of becoming a mother in addition to paid worker, I was made aware of the staggering extent of difference between the role expected from me and that expected from my partner. From the outset of pregnancy I was reminded, in subtle and not so subtle ways, that I was a mother now – even to the point of being called 'mummy' by one Sister in the antenatal clinic. I was overwhelmed from all quarters with advice, information, support, gifts and equipment on loan. My partner got none of this.

The medical profession continued this differentiated treatment. We were disappointed with how much the father's role was marginalized. The hospital's policy of encouraging fathers to attend the birth of their baby meant in practice that men were tolerated as long as they did not get in the way. The hospital, like many others, was insensitive to the needs of many women; for example, it had not recognized that some ethnic-minority women might be used to different cultural practices in childbirth, where the presence of women friends and relatives is preferable to that of prospective fathers.

After my child's birth I perceived a marked change in the

way I and the other mothers were treated. Our views no longer counted, and we were rushed into adopting the well-established practices of child care, such as breast-feeding. Fathers were kept at a distance; rigid visiting hours meant that they had less time with their babies and partners and missed the chances of bonding. I asked for Kiran's first bath, described by the nurse as a demonstration, to be delayed until his father was present, since he wanted to do the bathing at home. The request prompted much surprise and was ignored.

Taking Kiran to the local health clinic for weighing and to meet health visitors was also illuminating. Fathers who came with their partners and babies were rarely spoken to directly by staff – the assumption being that they were merely bystanders or 'chauffeurs'. The considerable number of Asian fathers who came were generally treated as interpreters only, so advice was prefaced by comments like 'Tell your wife she must . . .' Over a couple of years I became aware that many of these men were competent and willing carers of their own children. But the stereotyped view of Asian men 'oppressing their women' and having little to do with child care prevailed. This stereotype is harmful and insulting to men and women. I have witnessed more expressions of warmth, kisses and cuddles directed to Asian children by their fathers than I have ever seen shown by white fathers in Britain. I also have considerable experience of strong and assertive Asian women who are helping their own children break free from sex-role stereotypes. A friend told me once of the preferential treatment her husband received when he took their small daughter to the local health clinic for weighing. He was offered a small room to change her in private and congratulated on being 'so brave and clever' when he explained that he looked after their two children full-time and could easily manage a nappy change.

Assumption 2: the male sex is superior, so a boy child is preferred.

Though prospective parents are usually concerned about having a healthy, happy, well-adjusted baby who has few sleeping and eating problems, their attention is diverted by others on to one key issue: the desired sex of the baby. Parents are pushed to state a sex preference. Expressing preference for a girl surprises many, although this tends to be attributed to an act of perversity or a wish on the mother's part to have 'someone to dress up' and 'have as a companion'. Preference for a boy is accepted without the need for justification; after all, 'everyone wants the family line to continue'.

Much of the early child-care advice that parents receive hinges on the concept of sex difference and the importance of the male sex. Feeding a boy baby is expected to be done differently from feeding a girl – 'boys need more because they're more energetic'; 'you don't want a fat daughter'; 'he could do with a bit more fat on him, he's so puny'. A young boy who needs little sleep is excused by those not suffering from his wakefulness; after all, it's a sign that he is 'more intelligent and alert' and has an 'active mind'. A similarly wakeful girl is said to be 'difficult' and really must 'get her beauty sleep'.

In the early stages of life a baby may suffer from stomach pains, known as colic. Some specialists have claimed that only boys suffer this,

> as it is likely they are caused by the baby being lonely and tired and the realisation that he doesn't have his mother's full attention. Your thoughts have turned to getting a meal ready for your husband as is natural and seeing him.
>
> (Jolly and Gordon 1982)

The false assertion that girls do not suffer from this pain presumably stems from the idea that they will have learnt to cope with less attention already!

Elena Belotti (1975), Selma Greenberg (1979) and Judith Arcana (1983), among others, have considered the ways that the male sex is treated as superior in Western society. I shall focus on one way that language is used to this end: the commonplace practice in writing and speech of referring to the unknown child as 'he'. This happened to a friend when she went for an ultrasonic scan, late in her pregnancy. The radiographer used 'he' to refer to the baby and so she assumed the scan had revealed the sex. The radiographer laughed at this and said that it was usual practice to use 'he' because it was 'easier'. He was surprised by her suggestion that this could be misleading and disappointing.

'He', it is asserted by some baby-care writers, is used as a sex-inclusive term, which avoids the tedious use of 'she or he'. The idea of using 'she' like this is far too provocative. Jenny Cheshire has pointed out that

> there is a wealth of impressive evidence from psycho-linguistic experiments that when we are given a sentence containing the pronoun 'he' we interpret it as referring to a male subject, not a female one.
>
> (1985)

This interpretation is certainly the prevalent one made by young children. The way a baby behaves even in the womb gets interpreted in sex-stereotyped ways. So if that baby is consistently referred to as 'he', any kicking is interpreted as a sign that *'he's* going to be a footballer', never *'he's* going to be a dancer'.

Assumption 3: a child will be treated differently according to her or his sex.

This begins with the baby and affects all aspects of child care. Female and male babies and children are treated differently, and the myth of 'opposite sexes' is still prevalent (Greenberg 1979).

Assumption 4: boys and girls will develop differently from each other in behaviour, temperament, cognitive and physical ability.

Once different aspects of a child's character and behaviour are given social acceptance, it follows that children will stick with these aspects in order to maintain a good relationship with people in their environment – both authority figures and the peer group. Table 4.1 illustrates the different ways male and female babies and children are treated and are expected to behave.

TABLE 4.1   *Sex-stereotyped treatment of babies and young children*

AREA	BOYS	GIRLS
Sleeping patterns	Poor sleeping is excused and attributed to liveliness.	Girls need their 'beauty sleep'.
Crying	Not tolerated, therefore dealt with more readily to stop crying. Boys learn to suppress this expression of emotions early on (Belotti 1975).	Babies left to cry. Crying expected from girls and continued to a relatively late age.
Feeding	Given more breast-feed and for longer. Concern if they look underfed.	Given less, weaning earlier. Concern if they look overfed.
Physical play	Rough-and-tumble encouraged between boys and with adults. Assumed to be more active (Loo and Wenar 1971).	Treated with more care. Less adult male play. Assumed to be less active.
Signs of affection	Learn to shake hands not kiss. Affection shown to mother is more criticized the older the boy gets. Not liked if kisses other boys Can kiss girls and babies.	Encouraged to kiss everyone. Can show affection to mother till quite old. Approved if kisses other girls, babies and boys.
Use of outdoors	Encouraged to use space and be active (Hart 1978).	Less encouragement to play outside.

AREA	BOYS	GIRLS
Domestication	Help with car care, DIY, gardening; toys reflect this. Can be untidy.	Help with household chores; toys reflect this. Must be tidy.
Dependence/ independence	Encouraged to explore, not be 'tied to the apron strings'.	Kept close till older age (Belotti 1975, Hart 1978, Serbin 1979).
Socializing	Can be rough with other boys; 'like a gentleman' with girls.	Must be 'ladylike' with girls. Not to play with boys – 'they're too rough'.
Aggression/ assertiveness	Encouraged to 'avoid being a wimp'. A boy's aggression to another is a case of 'boys will be boys'.	Restrained, even if standing up for themselves.

Do the Children Have Any Say?

By the time children are two or three years old and can talk about themselves and their relationships with others, they have some awareness of the physical differences between people and are interested in how such differences relate to them. In conversation with my 2½-year-old I have noticed that he has observed differences between people in terms of size, age, skin colour, sex and physical ability. Fortunately he does not yet link these physical differences to judgemental assertion of do's and don'ts, can's and can'ts. Children's attention is drawn to differences and opposites by the songs and stories that they hear. Yet whilst promoting such a sense of difference, those involved with young children are coy and evasive in two areas: they tend to be 'colour blind', and avoid discussion of anatomical sex difference, yet happily create sex-role differences (Greenberg 1979).

In a very busy learning period children are subject to a

host of influences that preserve the status quo. The influence of the child's close family is strong, and so is that of the media and the peer group. The following three incidents illustrate some of the experiences my son has had from his contact with other children. In these encounters he is picking up messages about the type of behaviour that is socially acceptable for all children and what is expected of boys in particular, if they wish to join with their peers. Caution is needed before asserting that sex identification operates between peers (see Greenberg 1979), but we can at least give this source of influence consideration in connection with the adults' reactions and how these affect the bonds developing between children.

(1) Kiran and I had been going to a 'baby bounce' for several months at the local leisure centre. Towards the end of one session two four-year-old boys started to fight with another boy, pushing him to the ground and piling on top of him. This boy's carer reproved him for being 'all talk' and 'bottling out'. The adults with the other two just laughed, even louder when a younger brother started to make threatening postures. Kiran was bewildered by all this, but the following week he imitated the boys as he approached others.

(2) Children react differently depending on the setting – not only the physical environment, but also who is there. For example, one morning at our nursery co-operative Kiran and two young brothers were playing happily alongside each other with play-dough and animal shapes. Shortly after, two other boys arrived with toy guns (although we have a no-guns policy) and almost immediately started chasing, shouting and shooting each other. The whole atmosphere changed; both Kiran and his two friends reacted till all the boys were running about. There were confrontations, fights and tears, one gun was lost, the other broken.

We diverted the children's attention into a variety of other activites and by taking charge and splitting up the children we were able to restore the peace. I was struck by the change not only in Kiran and his friends but also in the others once parted from their guns and involved in more constructive play.

(3) Boys and girls in this nursery have marked out territories for themselves. Sometimes the same equipment or space is used in very different ways. A wooden framework that has a door and window is turned into a home or shop by groups of girls and becomes the setting for some imaginative and co-operative play; boys use it to hammer on, bang the doors and windows and fight over occupancy.

It is important to become aware of the conflicting messages that children pick up from their peers and to find ways of helping them understand just how complex any individual can be. Voicing concern over the aggression of a boy or the passivity of a girl is not enough. We must help children express their feelings – the whole range – and understand how non-productive aggression or passivity can be. We must also avoid making over-generalizations like 'he's so tough', 'always on the go', 'a good little fighter', 'she's so good-natured', 'home-loving', especially in their hearing. Remember that these are only characteristics children demonstrate some of the time.

We need also to be alert to the images that children are subjected to from the media. In Chapter 8 we discuss images in books and toys, and other writers have shown the influence of books and the media on children's attitudes and achievements (Maccoby 1966, Campbell and Wirtenberg 1978). In addition to children's programmes it is important to consider breakfast-time and early-evening television. Some violent and sexist US imports (*Dukes of Hazard*, *The A-Team*, etc.) have been screened earlier in the evening to catch a young audience, and this has been linked with the heavy promotion of toys featuring the fast cars, combat gear and guns seen on the programmes.

Over a period of several months' selective viewing of children's programmes (from both the BBC and commercial television) I have noticed a sexist bias in both programmes and advertisements, and a preponderance of violent themes, particularly in cartoons. By contrast, studio-based programmes that have an educational perspective – like

Playschool, Rainbow and *Mooncat* – are attempting a positive approach. Both men and women appear as informed, skilled and caring adults. Yet these positive gains are undermined by the cumulative effects of the other programmes on offer. Much of the material is dated, particularly the inevitable American cartoons with their superfluity of heroes or violent 'humanized' male animals, and as a consequence the sexist, racist and élitist values of an earlier generation are openly promoted.

Young children are treated daily to short-story series animated with puppets or illustrations (*Postman Pat, Camberwick Green, Alfie Atkins*, etc.). The majority of these use a male story-teller and have a male main character – apart from *Heggarty Haggerty*, which features a witch.

Advertisements shown during breakfast-time, early-evening and weekend children's programmes concentrate on toys, food, drinks and sometimes household commodities. They are heavily sex-biased. Dolls, cuddly animals and home-based toys – cookers, vacuum-cleaners and the like – are shown being played with by girls only. Boys alone are shown using cars, highly competitive games, bikes and toys of aggression. In food and drink advertisements boys of all ages are shown as rock stars and dancers; girls, when they are featured, are their adoring fans. Some animated images are openly racist, associating black characters with a jungle setting, rhythmic drum-beat and other such stereotypes. Needless to say, household commodities are still used only by women; they get 'expert' advice from a man, who appears in person or does the voice-over.

Strategies for change

1 Avoid describing characteristics as typically masculine or feminine. See the wide-ranging potential of every child, given encouragement and non-restricting treatment.
2 Remember (and remind others) that diversity between people operates within the same sex.
3 Remember (and remind others) that each individual has

a range of characteristics, behaviours, emotions and capabilities and will respond differently in different settings and with different people.

4 Try to offer an alternative, additional viewpoint when sexist comments are made.

5 Remember that you have time on your side. Your views, attitudes and behaviour will become apparent to your child as she or he gets older. You will remain the constant factor in your child's life.

6 Even when your own roles seem to reflect the traditional stereotypes, e.g. for economic reasons, try to point out to your child that alternative roles are possible.

7 Do not trivialize or elevate a role or task just because it is traditionally sex-associated (Bowman 1978).

8 Talk, talk, talk; share your views with your child, relatives, friends, professionals and other parents.

9 Be careful in the selection of experiences that you organize for your child. But be realistic that you cannot build a shell to protect your child.

10 Find ways to exert influence on the outside world. Unite with other parents and carers to express your view and change practice in shops, libraries, schools, health centres and playgroups. Express views in writing to pressure book publishers and booksellers, toy manufacturers, television programme editors and so on. Find support from established groups like women's centres and community bookshops.

Remember that children are human beings who have a right to express themselves and not just become a walking, talking version of your political beliefs:

> The active/passive, aggressive/submissive distinctions are not only traditional male/female distinctions. They also express values in a capitalist society . . . some parents may feel so strongly about non-sexism that they are prepared to enforce it in their children. Do we really want non-sexism at any price? How can we encourage non-sexism without being authoritarian, without thwarting our children's developing personality and autonomy?
>
> (Gender Rules OK 1978)

CHAPTER 5

Establishing co-operation between parents and staff: a parent's view

MINNIE KUMRIA

Until recently the issues of racism and sexism have been consistently ignored within British education. When in more recent times they have been considered, it is as though they are separate from and outside the class structure. On one hand, few people are aware of the difference between racialism (the individual reaction) and racism (institutional, legal, governmental). On the other, sexism has been treated as something of a joke. Meanwhile the oppression and exploitation of black workers and women are very real.

The successive Immigration Acts and the new Nationality Bill have made sure that there is a permanent section of our society who have fewer rights than others. Such laws have been used against black workers and particularly black women on numerous occasions. The 'virginity tests' enforced on Asian women arriving at Heathrow Airport a few years ago, the 'marriage of convenience' myths, the deportation of black and immigrant widows and divorcees with rights to stay in Britain, and the splitting and separation of families are but a few examples of institutionalized sexism and racism. To this we must add the history of exploitative wages, unsocial hours of work in unhealthy conditions, harassment at work by white male and female management and workers, lack of union representation and unions split along male/female, black/white lines. The picture is indeed a grim one.

How can we as parents hope to challenge the status quo in order to bring about sufficient change at the earliest stages of education, thus ensuring a better developed child, free of sexism and racism? As nursery education is the first step towards institutionalizing our children, it is important that parents participate at every possible level. This is the first stage where people other than parents (or equivalent) formally participate in the care of a child. It can also become the first step for the parent towards ultimate non-participation in a child's education, given the inherent relationship existing between parents and teachers.

Clashes of opinion between anti-sexist parents and child-minders are more easily resolved than those between parents and school staff. The child-minder has neither the authority nor the status that the 'professionals' can exert over parents. A child-minder is seen as a mother substitute, and hence parents see her as more of an equal. Also, as there is direct payment involved (though exploitative), parents feel more able to criticize.

The nursery school is also the stage at which new and different values are introduced to a child. Now the peer group of a child exerts enormous influence on her or him. The child/adult ratio is severely reduced from either home or the child-minding situation. The child/children ratio increases, and it is harder for parents to tackle the various views brought to school by other children. The narrow grouping of children by age range now takes place; this is in many ways unhealthy, limiting their concept of themselves in relation to the rest of society. Unless we as parents are both vigilant and participatory, our children will absorb values without challenge or question.

Given that there is far more contact between parents and staff at the nursery level than at any other within education, it is important that this contact be developed into co-operation towards achieving the same goal: a healthy, balanced person. Parents must establish their equal right in the development of their children at this stage, and as far as possible the children themselves should be consulted even at this young age. As a parent trying to teach her child non-sexist values, I know that my input in the world of my child is only a small one. All children to a greater or lesser extent come into contact with the ideas of the wider society – ideas that maintain the injustices of the status quo. These ideas are often perpetuated by nursery and school staff, who may be both overworked and lacking in awareness of the issues.

How then do we parents devise a methodology for co-operation and interaction with school staff for the benefit of our children? This chapter examines some of the possibilities in three main areas: parent–staff communication; the provision of learning materials; and staff training and attitudes.

New channels of communication

Most of the interaction that takes place between parents and teachers is within the school environment. As a mother in paid employment, I feel this is limiting, as there are few opportunities for women like me to participate. The hurly-burly atmosphere in a nursery is not conducive to any in-depth discussion. This also puts us at a disadvantage to take up issues, since we are aware that we do not come often enough to the school.

The first time I visited my son at his nursery, for example, the children were reciting nursery rhymes together as the last group activity of the day. I was horrified to hear my then 2½-year-old mouthing, 'The mums in the bus go natter, natter, natter . . . the dads in the bus go shush, shush, shush!' Women, who nowadays work at a wide variety of jobs, are still portrayed in the nursery as mindless gossips. I was deeply disturbed by this stereotyped concept of women and men, but felt unable to take up the issue with the teacher as I was aware of my lack of presence in the school. This reinforcement of sex stereotypes, added to the fact that we have fewer opportunities to make our views known in school, is indeed a matter for serious thought.

We ourselves as parents need to look closely at the extent to which we reinforce the stereotype of mothers as 'carers'. On the rare occasions when I have collected my son from school or taken him there, I have seen only one father doing the same. It is mothers only performing this – or child-minders: female. Even when both parents work, it is invariably the mother who rushes after work to pick up the child. We cannot hope to change the perception of our children unless we ourselves also put anti-sexist views into practice.

Meetings at School

There is no reason why more informal meetings, in smaller groups, cannot be brought about within schools, after school hours. Working mothers particularly would find this useful. To familiarize ourselves with the classrooms, the books and learning materials our children use would put us in a stronger position to take up issues that disturb us. We would start with information we need and should have.

Meeting in smaller groups of parents and teachers has many advantages. Firstly, speaking in large gatherings can be daunting. For women particularly, who may have rarely spoken in public, it can be very inhibiting because men have traditionally done the talking on such occasions. Parents in small groups can also share experiences and insights into their own and their children's home life. The Family Co-operation Project based at the ILEA Centre for Urban Education Studies included working with parents and staff in one multicultural school in Hackney, East London. The project workers visited parents at home as well as facilitating meetings in school and found that parents had considerable insight into the whole reading process and their children's abilities. Yet these were over-worked, black, bilingual parents, who are generally held in low esteem by school staff.

If you are challenging an age-old sexist issue, you are especially aware of the limitations of time. Large meetings are hardly the place to bring like-minded people together. Hence the need for smaller gatherings.

The children's own classroom should be used for school meetings, which would enable parents to make themselves familiar with the infrastructure used for teaching. If these classrooms were made available for a wider range of community activities, then a school could be a place that parents visited more freely, e.g. for English language classes or literary schemes, a place for learning skills from one another and from people in the locality. After the revolution in Grenada, parents were not only involved in physically constructing school buildings and devising curricula, but also made the buildings multi-functional. Just as the concept of libraries being the 'hallowed' buildings for quiet reading needs to be broken, similarly we must make multi-faceted use of schools for the benefit of the whole community. The barriers between home and school, parents and teachers must be broken down. Parents must be made to feel more welcome in schools.

Meetings at Home

As an alternative or addition to this, smaller meetings could also be arranged in parents' homes. This is again important in breaking down barriers between parents and staff as well as between parents, staff and children. In some cases a teacher will find that a mother is struggling to fight sexism in her own life and needs support if she is to fulfil some of her hopes for her child. Many parents are in some awe of teachers, but will talk with greater confidence on their own territory. Such meetings could thus be of great benefit to teachers in understanding a child and having some idea of the home environment. Parents would also have the opportunity to lay to rest the age-old myth that some staff hide behind: that parents are more sexist than the teachers themselves are; this is especially a cultural stereotype of black parents.

From a child's point of view this alternative for meetings can be highly productive. Visits from teachers add to a child's appreciation of the value of the home. For working and house-bound mothers there is little opportunity to participate in their child's education. Traditionally, women as mothers are seen by their children as providers and carers. Many of us who are trying to show our children that we are also individuals with other facets find it difficult to do so. Our children tend to see us only in the roles allotted to us by society. Creating the conditions where women can be seen to speak in their own right will generate a healthy respect in their offspring where none existed before. It would help too if some of these meetings took place without the menfolk. Most women (of *all* cultures) speak more freely without men around.

A home environment has the possibility of creating conditions where language and cultural barriers can be overcome, given the will to do so on both sides. In an age of high technology where information can be got at the touch of a button, communication through human contact – people meeting and getting to know each other – is fast losing its place. Yet such meetings in my view are irreplaceable. Given time and space, in addition to verbal communication, we communicate at a variety of levels. Mannerisms, gestures, levels of hospitality as well as the objects we surround ourselves with – all say something about ourselves to outsiders. A culture can be better understood by staff members if they visit a home that practises it. While seeing the differences, this also provides the opportunity to appreciate similarities between cultures.

Cultures in themselves are not barriers unless we make them so; many parents have made the effort to learn some English (there is no reason why this process cannot be reciprocated by staff), which they will feel less inhibited in trying out in their own home. The child concerned, and other children in the home, can be involved in interpreting; and a variety of other new possibilities open up.

Outings
Outings with parents as helpers are a recent move adopted by a growing number of schools. For many house-bound mothers such activities are a welcome opportunity to go out

as well as to meet other parents and children and communicate with different age groups. Few working parents can
participate, however, as a result of which their children
may also be left out. Usually it is the mothers who are
involved in outings, but they are an opportunity for men
also to participate and show themselves as 'carers'. In these
days of high unemployment for men, many of whose wives
are in low-paid part-time jobs, this is a chance for a useful
exchange of roles, ensuring their children's participation
too.

Written Communication
Many schools have information booklets or leaflets on
school life for new parents. It would be useful if this was
done by all schools and in multilingual versions. This
would go a long way in making parents feel more welcome
and show them that they are being thought of. If the same
were done for signs and directions within the school, the
gesture would be greatly appreciated and add to the
confidence of parents newly coming to school.

Most written communication between school and
parents is at the level of parents being informed individually of events and activities. Introducing a parents/school
newsletter could help in (1) collecting information and
(2) giving parents a forum for expressing and communi-
cating their views and ideas. Such a newsletter has the
potential to lead to all sorts of creativity and again should
be multilingual. Besides the joint effort of producing it, like-
minded parents and staff could reach out to one another at
different levels of interest and concern, both within and
outside school. Children's artwork could be reproduced
in it, giving them a feeling of involvement as well.

Selecting and producing learning materials

Arts and Crafts
The visual materials used and made in schools have a
profound significance for young people. Children's own

artwork, paintings and collages can give us – staff and parents – an insight into the thinking of our children and into the impact that we, and society at large, have on them. Moreover, because very little non-sexist and anti-racist visual material exists, this has to be produced – and can be done quite easily, drawing on the knowledge and experience of both parents and children.

How children easily integrate home and school, past and present experience in their artwork was recently seen in a collage produced by Bangladeshi children in a Bengali community project in the East End of London. There was Big Ben and the Houses of Parliament side by side with fishing boats on the banks of a river that could be the Thames or a river in Sylhet. Women, men and children in Eastern and Western dress walked happily amongst London buses, cows, buffaloes and cars. An Eastern sunset presided over the scene.

What came to mind was whether such a happy amalgam of ideas and talents would be possible in a school – as opposed to a community – environment, where racist views tend to inhibit the natural creativity of young children. It is surely no accident that such a piece of work came out of a community project where the children created in confidence and their work was encouraged and approved.

The use of embroidered, woven and printed fabrics in the form of wall-hangings, as well as artefacts from different parts of the world, all made by women, would have a joint anti-sexist and anti-racist impact, teaching the children a better respect for women as artists and creators. Such pieces can be used as a talking point, for teaching about different cultures and the richness they offer. Women as potters, weavers, artisans – particularly women from the developing countries – can be shown in a totally new and positive light; this will go a long way in countering the myths that have emerged about them.

Parents, particularly mothers, can be drawn into putting such materials together with the staff. Many of us have a wealth of information on such products, which could enrich learning for our children. In fact, many mothers are

themselves skilled in some of these arts and could be drawn
into practical demonstrations. When, for example, tie-dye
was being developed for the under-fives in one West
London nursery, a Nigerian mother came up with some
very useful suggestions, like putting pebbles, seeds and
marbles in between ties, which young children could easily
do. She was very pleased to be invited in to demonstrate to
all the children, and was especially popular with them.

Block printing is another simple activity through which
designs from different cultural sources can be introduced.
The possibilities are endless.

Visual Material

It is crucially important that from the youngest age children
be exposed to visual material showing women and girls,
and men and boys, in untraditional, non-stereotypical roles
– be they at work or in the home. Pictures of the women and
girls need to reflect different cultures and classes, thus
breaking down racist, sexist and élitist myths.

Aspects of different cultures when shown in comparison
with one another become more meaningful, and the exotic
element, which is stressed in isolation (consciously or
otherwise), can be removed. A few years ago the National
Association for Multicultural Education in London put
together some excellent visuals in which subjects such as
'head-dress' and 'body painting' were included. They
countered racist and exotic concepts, and challenged views
of what is right or wrong, acceptable or not, and from
whose point of view. 'Head-dress' featured women and
men wearing hats and caps of different shapes, sizes and
colours in Europe, African and Asian turbans, scarves and
sari *pallous* (one end of a sari) covering the head; all were
shown as evolving within cultures as a result of tradition or
practical reasons, such as protection against the weather.
'Body painting' showed the variety of colours that the
Western woman uses on her face, as well as colours used by
women and men in other cultures for the same reasons of
either beautification or cultural tradition. Because compari-
sons were made and contexts were shown in these visuals,

the non-European fashions and traditions looked neither
ludicrous nor exotic.

In producing visual materials, it helps to remember that
what we are trying to do is (1) portray realities of life in
general and (2) teach our children *not* to be stereotypical.
For example, instead of replacing a white woman by a black
woman who is still in a kitchen, if we show a black woman
on a construction site, say, we broaden a child's horizons
much more. Women in India and elsewhere really do hard
manual work in construction.

Music, Dance and Theatre

This is an area that has been grossly under-used in the
development of our children. Rhythm and movement come
naturally to most children and are a source of great enjoy-
ment, besides developing a unique set of skills. Introducing
musical instruments such as thumb pianos, flutes and
different types of drums, or even making simple instruments such as shakers, can teach children a great deal about
their multicultural world.

Dance is another area where sexist stereotypes need to be
broken down. It has been considered 'cissyish' to dance.
My son's enthusiastic gyrations to any type of music are
entirely his creation. To this I have slowly added hand-
gestures depicting birds flying, deer running, a bee sucking
nectar from a flower, fish swimming; such movements are
common in Indian dancing and are an added dimension to
something he enjoys.

Story-telling

Story-telling depicting girls in roles of leadership, women
from history, women as freedom fighters and suffragettes
can be put on to cassettes. Even sexist folk-tales and fairy
stories can be modernized and changed. Animal stories
particularly, which are so popular with young children and
persist in the use of the pronoun 'he' when referring to
wolves, lions and jackals and 'she' when talking about
rabbits and other small furry creatures, can be changed
round quite easily.

Parents of different cultures can be involved in story-telling in schools, where direct interaction can take place between them and the children. The use of a few artefacts can make the experience more exciting as well as teach something about another culture. I have successfully experimented with bilingual story-telling in Bengali and English to the same group of children at a book event. The response was amazing; not only did the white children listen to the Bengali version with great attention, but the Bangladeshi children were thrilled to hear their own language spoken. The rapport was amazing; I was told later by one of the teachers that she had never heard the children talk so much.

Parents writing and illustrating story-books can also present more positive images of women and different races and cultures.

Recipe Cards

All children enjoy creative activities, and cooking is certainly one of them. Simple recipes from different cultures that involve only a few easy stages of putting a few ingredients together and mixing them can be a very rewarding experience. Introducing simple cooking at school can also go a long way in countering the stereotype that only women and girls cook. Recipe cards showing the different stages involved in visual form, together with a picture of the complete dish, are easy to produce and add to the children's interest.

Toys and Games

Many of the toys and games that are on the market make some dangerous assumptions, either in just their visual presentation or in their content or in both. At least one construction set has a picture of a little boy *only* playing with the toy. The assumption of the manufacturer is that anything involving screwdrivers, spanners, nuts and bolts can be of interest only to boys. The product itself is excellent, and girls would enjoy making and fixing things as much as boys do.

Another famous brand of educational toys (Lego) is similarly guilty of stereotyping girls and boys. I recently picked up a simple box containing about fifteen pieces that, when put together, constructed a vehicle on wheels, with a girl and boy as passenger and driver respectively. On bringing it home and constructing it, we discovered that the pieces were made in such a way that the boy had to be the driver and the girl the passenger. Only with great difficulty (and well beyond the skills of a four-year-old, for whom this was intended) could you change the figures around. At this point my son plucked the girl figure out, as the picture on the box showed the boy driving.

These are just two examples of the ease with which children can he channelled into stereotyped role-playing by toy manufacturers. It is not enough to present all toys to all children; we must become positively involved when they are being played with, if we are to counter the stereotypical roles perpetuated through them.

Jigsaws that introduce different views of women and men, black and white, and pick and stick games, can easily be produced. A small number are already commercially available.

Play-Acting and Role-Play

The play-acting and role-play adopted by children tell us a great deal about their development and what they imbibe from their worlds. Sex roles within society, in the home and at school, are duplicated with frightening accuracy. As adults, we can see our actions and behaviour patterns repeated in our children's role-play, which, if observed carefully, can act as a sharp reminder to correct our wrong methods before it is too late.

The interaction between aware adults and children in role-play can effectively challenge both racist and sexist ideologies. In a home, who does the housework, cooking, disciplining, etc. has an effect on the awareness of a child. Not just the preference for certain toys but the way they are used will reflect societal power structures in the perception of that child; both may be guided by an aware adult.

After voicing the opinion that 'dads don't make dinner' at 2½, my son at 3 not only stopped making such observations but now actively participates in cooking at weekends. It was also heartening to hear that when our child-minder's son (who is white) presented her with a make-believe 'cup cake', our son made her a *paratha* (a form of Indian bread). His initial statement, though based on the stereotypical roles observed outside our home, led us as parents to double our efforts in countering it. It is also reassuring that when we as a family participate in my son's play-acting, my husband and I are often given roles contrary to our sex and age.

It is common to see children taking on the roles of their favourite TV characters. For every Wonderwoman, there are a host of males – Superman, Mr T., Knight Rider, He-Man, etc. These pop heroes exist side by side with cartoon characters and with folk-tale personalities like Hansel and Gretel in our children's world. In every instance, the stories and the characters reinforce the aspects of stereotyping that we are trying to break down. Very little challenging of these sex roles takes place so far in schools. In 'dressing-up' play, boys rush around being Superman in capes; girls play at 'prettying up' and going to parties, wearing the same capes. Passive and active roles are adopted even in the clothes chosen.

It is possible to enter this world of make-believe and, by changing the characters, break down the sexual and racial bias that is symbolized by them. Further, by introducing everyday clothes from different cultures, we can remove the 'exotic' view of them and the people who wear them. Familiarizing children with these can go a long way in countering myths about people of other cultures than their own.

Similarly, house-play equipment tends to focus on traditional female-associated tasks: cooking, ironing, washing, shopping. However, it could easily include decorating tools and equipment associated with hobbies, which girls as well as boys could be encouraged to use.

Selecting materials together can be an important learning

process for parents and staff. As many of us experience parenthood as an exploratory situation, it is important to pool our information and discoveries. Jointly we can put pressure on manufacturers and publishers regarding not only the visual presentation of their products but also the contents of the products themselves.

Staff training and teacher attitudes

Institutionalized racism and sexism, as seen in Britain today, are also reflected in education at the teacher-training level. Instead of being an integral part of *all* training for teachers, any awareness of both these issues is taught in 'optional' courses – as though they are peripheral and not fundamental attitudes to be earnestly tackled. The educational system contents itself by making gestures towards rectifying things through in-service training courses.

Based on my own and other parents' (and parent-teachers') experience of negative attitudes and a serious lack of information among staff, I feel that insights like the following need to be the content of teacher training initially and in service.

Taking a Positive Stand

Recently I visited my son's nursery and was discussing the issue of sexism with a member of staff. She made the point that *all* the toys were given to *all* the children to play with. Yet I could see the children playing sexist roles. Positive participation and suggestion were clearly needed from staff in order to break down the pre-defined sex roles that were being enacted.

We need to remind ourselves that we are trying to break down the stereotypes within society. We need to be seen and heard doing this. We have to actively encourage girls and boys to see toys, games, jobs, chores and tastes free from sex roles. We have to try to undo in school what they may be learning from the media and from the rest of society. The attitudes that are being perpetuated are the object of our attack.

Nursery-school staff need to have a knowledge of the history, culture and linguistic heritage of the diversity of people who have made Britain their home. Staff need to establish more sensitive relations with parents. In essence this means establishing better relations between two groups of women: white, English, middle-class staff and mothers who include black, working-class women. We cannot talk about anti-sexist education within school without also looking at the existing sexist and racist attitudes adopted towards mothers, black mothers particularly. Being patronizing towards parents from countries other than their own is relatively common among staff. This is then carried further when dealing with the children.

Many nursery and teaching staff reveal a desire to cling to their 'professionalism' and preserve their status *vis-à-vis* parents. The mystique that surrounds professions such as medicine and law is also common to nursery teaching; but having acquired a specialized skill does not in any way make doctors, lawyers or teachers superior to, or wiser than, parents. Teachers choose to forget, ignore or belittle our tremendous expertise; we have cared for our children, one or more, for twenty-four hours a day. We have relevant information on our cultures and languages, the knowledge and skills achieved through the work we do and the occupation we follow.

Many teachers expect parents to make moves to come to understand the complexities of new trends in education – e.g. learning through play, the new maths, new reading and writing methods. Yet how many teachers are willing to recognize the diverse experiences of their class-children and really learn about the cultures they will encounter through them?

A Sense of History
Women in general and black women in particular have been in the forefront of many struggles, be it against

colonial domination or cultural oppression. Every non-sexist and anti-racist approach to teaching and nursery work must be based on this fact.

Why have people of such diverse backgrounds made Britain their home? Is it out of choice, because of economic necessity, because of Britain's need for cheap labour? Is immigration to Britain an extension or result of colonial oppression and exploitation? What impact does this have on the women of a particular community? Does immigration disrupt the cultural pattern of that society? Does it weaken or strengthen the position of the women concerned? What was the status of these women in their homelands? Does living in smaller social groupings in a hostile white society have a progressive or retrogressive impact on the position of women and girls? Are changes taking place (for the better or not) in the homelands that are not reflected among different cultural groups living in Britain? If not, why not?

Cultures are dynamic entities and can best be understood within the context of history. Without a historical understanding of a people, the celebration of its cultural diversity (e.g. festivals) degenerates into meaningless symbolism, which conveys nothing of lasting impact.

Sexism exists in all cultures and all societies. Because of industrialization and the uneven development of societies due to colonialism, some issues have been challenged and won by some women while others are still struggling against them. However, (1) all women are aware of their oppressions; none of them need telling how to wage their struggles; (2) all sexism is unacceptable and must be tackled on that basis and no other.

The élitism of white women emerges strongly when dealing with black mothers. Much of it is based on preconceived notions of the oppression of black women through their patriarchal culture. This leads white women to perpetuate sexist stereotypes of both black women and men. Generalized assumptions are made; passive Asian women and domineering men are seen as part of a cultural norm; West Indian homes are thought of as made up of one-parent families where usually either the mother or father is nowhere around.

Some white female teachers are even shocked when these stereotypes are not conformed to in school. For example, when watching a particular video of under-fives in their class, teachers invariably call one Bangladeshi girl domineering, even bossy, when she initiates an activity and organizes all the children, boys and girls. When two children – this same girl and a boy – are treated in equally caring fashion by a teacher, who sits them on her knee to share a book with her, teachers watching the video invariably criticize the 'babying' treatment of the boy, but never mention that of the girl.

White women must remember that we black women are aware of our oppression and are capable of waging our own struggles. Cultural oppression and sexism are best tackled by the women who are within them. We need to be supported in these struggles, but not constantly 'taught'.

Ignorance of religions, foods, wearing apparel and ways of living leads to the insensitive handling of children and situations. For example, children are still reprimanded by some adult helpers for eating with hands, not using knives and forks properly. There is the case of a little girl of Indian background who had refused to communicate with anyone at school. Her teacher's sensitivity and awareness of her culture helped in breaking down barriers when her gestures of flipping an imaginary thing between her hands were recognized as making a *chapathi*. In one class a boy dressed in a *lungi* was laughed at as wearing a dress. Fortunately the teacher was sensitive and aware enough to handle this properly.

The Celebration of Festivals in School
Celebrating religious and cultural events in school serves little purpose and brings children into only superficial contact with cultures other than their own. This is especially the case with the under-fives, who are too young to cope with the concepts embodied in the concrete story format. Though these celebrations may well form an

important part of the culture concerned, when presented in a static form, emphasizing the exotic and different aspects, they bring no change at all in attitudes. If our children are to grow up free of racism and sexism, then they have to be provided with the tools with which to counter them.

What, then, are we trying to achieve when we celebrate such events in school?

1 Are we trying to introduce children to an aspect of a different culture? Why? Is it possible to do so unless the peoples of that culture have been part of the learning process of those children? What work has been done around the subject to enable the children to grasp the essence of that culture and people in terms other than the exotic?

2 Are the contents of such celebrations loaded with sexist concepts? Do they in fact counter our efforts towards anti-sexist education? If so, why are they taking place?

Children themselves are a powerless component within a power structure that has also placed black and women workers at the bottom of the ladder. We cannot hope to change this structure unless we work to change it on a daily basis. Celebrating the Caribbean Carnival or the Chinese New Year may well make the children of those particular cultures feel important on that day; but what of all the other days? What is the self-perception of such children on a daily basis? How have we succeeded in making the other children more aware and respectful of them?

The only way we can make such celebrations a positive means of education is by involving the parents and community. The celebration must be seen within the context of that community and not in isolation. If such contact and communication exist between parents and staff, then the celebration will convey more to the children than merely the festival itself. The spirit of such occasions can be brought alive only by the people to whom it is meaningful. Its importance and relevance can be established only through ongoing contact between the groups concerned.

As things stand, there is an over-concentration on Christian festivals and celebrations even in state schools. Parents of other faiths should by right be informed of this; they can remove their children from such celebrations. Further, where celebrations from other cultures are included, the active roles tend to be given to boys, e.g. being part of the dragon in Chinese New Year, wearing the dragon's head to dance in, playing musical instruments, while girls 'pretty up' and form the entourage. We need to look closely at this issue. Unfortunately, all religions portray men as dynamic beings, with women either relegated to the background or as exotic creatures; but there are lesser-known stories in all religions that portray women otherwise. It would be useful to take away the 'superhuman' element in any case, and also to draw parallels between everyday life and these stories to make them more realistic for young people.

The existing involvement of parents in such celebrations amounts to yet another example of stereotyped role-playing. The fathers/males are usually the ones who inform the school/staff about the concepts behind religious acts, with strong male interpretations, with the mothers/women making the food, clothes, etc. that the children bring to school. This too needs to change.

Linguistic Heritage

Many of our children do not have English as a first language. Language is an integral part of any culture; ideas and concepts are conveyed through the language concerned. Mothers are still primarily responsible for child care, and as many of us do not have English as our stronger language, a child coming to a day centre or nursery may well communicate only in the first language. The linguistic difference is often treated as a sign of inferiority and hence a subject of contempt.

The process of alienation between mother and child can start here. Children often refuse to talk to mothers in nurseries because they fear contempt or ridicule. Mothers can get very isolated if they do not find means to communicate with people in a nursery. Some staff tend to assume that if someone doesn't talk (due to language differences) it is because they have no ideas or views, nothing to offer. This assumption is made more about bilingual women than about the men.

If women do find others who share their language at school, then they are sometimes belittled by staff. For example, Bangladeshi mothers talking together in one nursery were described to a visiting teacher as 'constantly yattering away'. Language is trivialized and mimicked, even by children. Bilingual women must have a forum for expressing their ideas in the language in which they are most comfortable.

It is essential that staff have a basic knowledge of the language concerned. Taking this a stage further, it is also essential that the names of children be pronounced correctly. Distorting a name or abandoning it and replacing it with another more suitable to the monolingual white tongue, or easier for administrative reasons, is not acceptable. In addition, to assume that a child's second name ('surname') is always the same as the parents' does not take into account different naming traditions.

There is a certain amount of pressure put on children and parents to speak 'proper' English, ignoring colloquialisms common to some cultures. This process has been known to so erode a child's confidence so much that she or he doesn't speak at all in school. Even such basic information about our backgrounds can bridge existing communication gaps between staff, children and parents.

Summary and conclusions

What parents can do to help staff:
1 Give insights about their own childhood, early learning process and child care.
2 Inform on cultural and religious events and individual life-style.
3 Practical help in a curriculum: stories, art, craft, cookery, music, dance, games, maths.

4 Help in selecting, developing and maintaining learning
  resources.

What staff can do to help parents:
1 Regular contact about child's development in school.
2 Ideas on continuing learning process.
3 Information on 'school culture', curriculum, resources.
4 Collaboration on resources, influencing publishers and
  toy manufacturers.
5 Support information on services in Britain: benefit
  system, hospital procedures, etc.
6 Support with tackling racism and sexism.

Many parents are aware of the needs and abilities of their
children. Many of us are also taking an anti-sexist stand in
our own lives in the belief that this is the only way forward.
Teachers need to look at the sexism and racism that they
practise and perpetuate towards both the children in their
care and those children's parents. Teachers, parents and
children can all learn from one another – but for this to
happen, conditions of equality and trust need to be established. Changing attitudes is a long process, but unless this
is consciously done on a continuous basis we cannot hope
to improve the quality of education for our children.

CHAPTER 6

Parental involvement: some feminist issues

NAOMI EISENSTADT

This chapter is written from a personal perspective. I see it as an opportunity to explore some of the dilemmas I have been caught in during ten years of working with the under-fives. These dilemmas arise from always having to identify with one or another of a variety of pressure groups, but always finding myself distinctly uncomfortable with the company. This is a common feature of political life, but it seems that few people working with young children realize how deeply political many of the issues are. This chapter explores issues concerned with parental involvement. I am both a feminist and a fierce defender of parental involvement, which for some women may seem contradictory. In defining parental involvement, I explain why it is seen by some to be anti-feminist. I further argue that while the styles of involvement promoted by many groups are indeed anti-feminist, this is not inherent in all models. I suggest that anti-sexist pre-school programmes can themselves be anti-feminist if they implicitly devalue or insult the mothers of the children participating in such programmes.

The anti-feminist argument

For feminists, there are two strong objections to parental involvement in pre-school settings:

1 The lack of adequate inexpensive day care is probably the single most important impediment to equal opportunities for women. Most centres that argue strongly in favour of involving parents do not provide full day care, and are therefore not offering the service that meets the needs of women who want to work full-time.
2 Implicit in the encouragement of parents to participate is an affirmation of traditional sex roles. 'Parent' almost always means 'mother'. Involvement is almost always seen as proof of performing adequately as a mother or as a means, for those who are having difficulty, to improve their mothering skills.

The two types of pre-school provision that argue most loudly for parental involvement are playgroups and family centres. Neither offer services that are well suited to working mothers. Playgroups, the major provider of services in the voluntary sector, were started as a self-help form of provision by mothers. Their short hours and heavy reliance on volunteers make them inconvenient even for women wishing to work part-time.

Many family centres were originally day nurseries, which did provide a comprehensive and subsidized day-care service, albeit for women fitting into certain categories of need. For some centres, in changing from day nurseries to family centres, hours were changed, numbers of children catered for were reduced, and a condition of getting a place was an agreement from the mother to be present some of the time. Hence the push towards involving parents in family centres actually reduced the already stretched provision for young children whose parents work.

The second objection to parental involvement concerns the inherently sexist assumptions underlying many programmes that seek to include parents. The most common models of parental involvement – those espoused by the Pre-school Playgroups Association, by most family centres and by many of those nursery classes and schools that do include parents – all carry an implicit message to women about their appropriate role as mothers. Their primary and most important task is child care. Moreover this task not only involves the basic practical skills of feeding, clothing and cleaning young children, it is increasingly being interpreted as involving the more complex tasks of adequate stimulation, promoting social skills and providing emotional stability (Perkins and Morris 1979). Perhaps of greater concern, many of the schemes assume a 'deficit model'; they operate on the assumption that some women are inadequate mothers and that the purpose of involvement is to improve their parenting skills. This not only results in women losing confidence, but also wastes the enormous resource of the skills and knowledge parents do have to offer.

Playgroups in recent years have been caught between the image of 'ordinary mums' coping beautifully with running their own services, and that of a voluntary social-work agency, providing non-threatening informal support for isolated mothers. While both of these images are accurate for some playgroups, there are considerable difficulties in performing both these roles, and both are questionable from a feminist point of view. As pointed out by Finch (1984b), the playgroup movement is supported by many influential writers, e.g.Penelope Leach (1979) and Mia Kelmer Pringle (1980) because it offers the model they consider most beneficial for women and children; that is, a rich and rewarding experience of full-time mothering.

Finch's critique rests not only on the implicitly antifeminist message of playgroups, but also on their essentially middle-class nature. The limited resources of working-class areas make the adoption of the self-help model inappropriate. Often the successful playgroups in middleclass areas are run by teachers or nursery nurses who have left work to raise their own children. Likewise, the finances may be administered by a member of the group who had relevant professional training before leaving work. Groups in middle-class neighbourhoods thus benefit from the wealth of education and experience of the community from which they draw their children. Working-class areas generate very different skills, but rarely ones that fit so conveniently into conventional styles of pre-school provision. To expect such abilities is unreasonable; to explain the failure of groups in working-class areas as a result of the 'inadequate' or at best less than diligent parenting of working-class mothers is grossly unfair.

The justification and aims for involvement in much pre-school provision rest on this model of parental inadequacy. Many family centres that encourage parents to participate do so as a means of therapy for the mother. Often the basis for a child's placement in a centre is some assessment of family difficulty. The explicit aims of many centres are concerned with helping the family to cope: improving parenting skills, improving relationships between parent and child, even 'mothering' the mother. Women become clients identified for some treatment because they are not adequately fulfilling their role as mother. As a feminist I would argue that it is the modern role of 'mother' that is inappropriate. It is no surprise that women in poverty, who are almost always the recipients of such care, are more prone to depression and stress (Brown and Harris 1978). The messages put forth in current early-childhood circles present successful mothering as a truly daunting task, requiring a knowledge of child development and psychology. Inadequate mothering is assumed to result in long-term serious consequences for children. Moreover, poverty itself makes it much more difficult for some women to fulfil the role. Lack of money denies many women the resources so often extolled by the protectors of motherhood as enriching and stimulating for both mothers and children (Leach 1979).

Working-class women are known to have higher illness rates than those from the middle class. They are also known to use health services, particularly preventive services, less. Granham (1984) argues that the fault lies not with the inadequacy of the mother, but rather with the poor organization and often distant location of the services available to her, which make them unsuitable for women with more than one child and no transport. Conversely, if services are flexible and responsive to their own consumers, they are likely to be over-subscribed.

Schools are also often guilty of a patronizing and judgemental version of parental involvement. Nursery classes will sometimes justify involving mothers as a means of showing them 'how it is done'. Mothers are cast in the role of pupils to learn from professional staff how more effectively to stimulate their children (Smith 1980). Tizard and Hughes (1984) have eloquently challenged the view that mothers need such training. Indeed, they found richer language in working-class home between mothers and daughters than between teachers and the same children in nurseries. The common core of shared experience between mothers and children fostered much more dialogue than the nursery staff, professionally trained to encourage language development, could stimulate. Likewise Wood *et al.* (1980) found that playgroup staff who lived in the same neighbourhood as the children in their care had more frequent extended conversations, often relating to shared experiences out of school. The staff whose knowledge was limited to the children's lives at playgroup were much more limited in their success at extending children's language.

The partnership model

As a feminist I fundamentally agree with all these criticisms of parental involvement. While I agree with Miriam David (1985) that most forms of involvement share an underlying affirmation that women's place is in the home, as a practitioner rather than a social scientist I ask the somewhat harder question: what should be offered? The answer cannot be simply more statutory services. While an expansion of the services is clearly needed, a radical change in the organization and management of services is also essential. Contraction has served one important function; it has forced many new initiatives and new styles of work to be implemented. It would be sad if a regeneration of under-fives services did not reflect some of the lessons learned from these innovations.

The high demand for traditional nursery classes and day nurseries in working-class areas is surely a result of their familiarity, and not an expression of complete consumer satisfaction. Traditional services are themselves very judgemental. They engender in their users feelings of guilt, inadequacy and, particularly for low-income women, powerlessness. A partnership model of parental involvement, on the other hand, does not exploit women's feelings of guilt, but reinforces some notion of control. This parental involvement model rests on a basic principle of community work: that consumers of public services have a right to share the control of those services with the workers who are paid to run them. This model of genuine partnership is rare; but having worked in just such a setting, I staunchly defend it on both political and pragmatic grounds.

A model of parental involvement that genuinely shares responsibility and power with parents carries with it some very different underlying assumptions from the self-help or inadequacy models previously discussed. In summary, these unsatisfactory models offered women three unacceptable choices:

1 Playgroups – do it all yourself: finance, premises, play activities, registration. Failure reflects on you as a parent and on your community.
2 Family centres – we will counsel you, help you with your problems, give you self-confidence, enable you to cope better as a mother.
3 Nursery school – learn from us. We know what young children need. We will teach you so you can teach him or her.

In contrast, the underlying principles of a partnership model are:

- People's choices, whether to stay home with young children or to go to work, are based on their own assessment of what is best for them. Therefore we cannot assume that those services not providing full day care are of no use to any mothers.
- Consumers of a service are usually well placed to know what they want from it. Service providers must be more open to consumer demands rather than trying to offer a service based on their perceptions and assessment of people's needs.
- If workers approach individuals with the expectation that they are competent and capable, those individuals can make a considerable positive contribution to services. Professionals often expect working-class women to have problems. That negative expectation colours their interaction and impedes co-operation.

Why is power not shared?

It is a sad irony that the nursery workers who most often devalue and criticize the abilities of women at home with young children are themselves caught in low-paid, low-status, predominantly female employment with a poor career structure. Perhaps because most under-fives workers are themselves so low in status within their own agency they feel they must jealously guard whatever expertise they have. Within the limited scope of looking after young children the only people who 'know less' than the paid carers are the unpaid carers, the mothers themselves. It can be highly threatening for staff, who themselves lack confidence, to share control with mothers.

It is even sadder and more frustrating that as a few men do trickle into family-centre work they do so only at senior level. Some family centres now require a social-work qualification for their leaders, making it more difficult for very experienced women who have been working in such settings for years to get leader posts. Similar to the preponderance of men in headships in primary schools, where the staff is mostly all female, it is increasingly common to find young male social workers running family centres almost entirely staffed by women. Often these men have only a very limited background in working with the under-fives and a lack of practical experience in caring for young children, making them inappropriate leaders for staff as well as clients.

For professionals lacking in confidence, it is often in their best interest to exaggerate family difficulties. It is a useful tool when trying to explain why a child has made very little progress – 'What do you expect? The mother never talks to her. There are no books at home. The TV is on all the time.' It is also more rewarding for the worker when substantial progress is made. Parents are an easy scapegoat for difficulties, but are rarely given the credit for improvements.

How a partnership model works

Much of what has been said in this chapter is based on my own observations and experience. I worked for five years in a family centre on a low-income estate in Milton Keynes. A playgroup on the same estate struggled with many of the difficulties described earlier that often plague playgroups in poor areas. The family centre I was involved with could be the target for some of the feminist criticisms outlined above. No, we could not offer full day care; yes, we did expect parents to spend time in the nursery class; places in the nursery were allocated on a criterion of need. Nevertheless, certain features of this centre were fundamentally different from the models described above, and there are other centres elsewhere run along similar lines. There are some playgroups, family centres and nursery schools and classes that involve parents in such a way as to empower them rather than turning them into children. It is the salient features of this type of practice that I wish to explore; I consider this type of parental involvement inherently feminist.

Moorland Centre offers two 24-place nursery classes, a

drop-in centre five mornings a week, a toy library and a variety of parent groups. It is financed by the Milton Keynes Development Corporation. The centre has three nursery workers, a home visitor, two drop-in workers and a centre leader. It is run by a management committee, the majority of whose members are parents who use the centre. The committee determines centre policy, criteria for nursery places, staffing and finance. Parents are elected to the committee at the Annual General Meeting. Usually about 60 per cent of parents attend the AGM, and there are always more candidates for the committee than vacancies.

The kinds of decision that parents are involved in are similar to the ideal playgroup self-help model: staff selection, finance, charges to parents, etc. However, adequate funding from an outside body prevents some of the confidence-destroying struggle of playgroups in poor areas. Further, it means that those who have a clear view about what kind of service should be on offer – the users themselves – are helping to determine it.

Power is genuinely shared, in that decisions at Moorland Centre sometimes go against the centre leader, the funding agency or the parents. Money is not unlimited, so the constraints are clear. However, because everyone knows where the limits are, they can make priorities co-operatively, using everyone's perceptions and experience constructively.

It is difficult to gauge the extent to which those parents on the committee represent the users or the community. The danger of working so closely and co-operatively with some parents is that others may feel excluded. An important function of professional staff in this setting is to ensure all parents are encouraged to participate at some level and to make sure the centre remains welcoming to new users.

Very few under-fives centres involve parents to this extent in management. Sometimes local-authority structure and regulation do not allow it. Moorland's attitude to individual parents is also somewhat unusual. No records are kept on drop-in users. The drop-in is an open community facility. Only the numbers of users coming in every day are recorded. The nursery keeps records on the children but they are open to parents, and assessments on children are reviewed with parents. No information on child or parent is passed to other agencies without the parent's permission.

It is also recognized that all families experience stress at some time. Whatever prompted the intake of a child to the nursery, situations change, get better or worse. While it is always tempting to ascribe improvements to the centre, crises do pass, and one never knows if the same improvements wouldn't have happened without intervention.

It is precisely this sharing of common experience and affirmation of personal strengths that can make parental involvement so enriching for women who are coping in difficult circumstances. The demands of involvement ('What can you give us?') rather than the assumptions of failure ('How can we help you?') enable and empower women, who are so unused to people treating them with respect. Many women have to cope not only with the stress of raising young children on a very low income, but also with the often judgemental and patronizing attitudes of health visitors, social workers, and nursery staff. No wonder services are often rejected by the very target group for whom they were intended.

There are some inherent difficulties and tensions in working so closely with parents. On the community level, while centre workers are willing to share power with centre users, they actually have very little power themselves. They must work with health visitors, teachers and social workers. At Moorland relationships are sometimes strained because of the centre's refusal to pass information about families without their permission. It is often this sharing of details about 'cases' that gives services, particularly in the voluntary sector, status and recognition from statutory workers. Such recognition helps the centre to run effectively alongside other local services and is important for the self-esteem of the staff. Positive relationships with colleagues who are working with the same families are sometimes strained when there is disagreement not only on the solutions to problems, but also on the context and definition of the difficulties.

On a more practical level, the combined role of working with children and adults can be difficult. Particularly in the drop-in, there can be confusion about whose role it is to discipline children and about appropriate forms of discipline. Workers are often torn between the stress of tolerating what they perceive as 'bad practice' and the need to be open and non-judgemental. There can be pressures from other parents to deal with mothers who continually smack or shout at their own children because it creates an unpleasant atmosphere for all users. The other women might exclude or isolate such a mother. The worker faces several dilemmas about the most positive action in terms of the individual and the group. There are no simple answers to such difficulties, and each must be dealt with as it arises. An acknowledgement that such issues are part of parental involvement is essential for workers in this setting.

This type of involvement is implicitly feminist because it acknowledges and affirms the demands and attitudes of women, a group of women largely ignored or dismissed by the mainstream feminist movement. The three issues that best illustrate the tensions of working as a feminist in such a setting are:

1 What about working women?
2 What about women who themselves believe in a traditional model?
3 What about anti-sexist programmes in the centre?

Some community nurseries have successfully combined parental management with day care. These centres are run by management groups and are subsidized by employers. They reflect excellent co-operation between staff and management in industry but are under financial threat because the government considers such subsidies to be taxable perks. Taxing subsidized day care would make it financially disadvantageous to work for many parents who use these centres.

Moorland does not offer day care. It does offer support

for local child-minders through the toy library, the drop-in and a Child-minders' Group. Nursery parents who find work while their child is attending are helped to find a minder who would be willing to drop off and collect the child for the half-day session. Such a minder is invited to participate in lieu of the parent, and of course may bring her own children.

Child-minding is itself poorly paid, isolating and exploitative. However, a centre like Moorland can improve conditions somewhat, and is helping the working parent to find some form of day care. The increased costs and reduction in numbers of children that would have resulted from offering day care could not be carried within the existing structure. In fact, probably due to the poor employment opportunities in the area, it was a demand not often made.

Many parents themselves do not want to work while their children are very young. Some of the women I knew had evening cleaning jobs, so that they could generate some income while keeping primary care of the children.

'I don't believe in women's lib'

The reality for many women is that their main area of expertise and self-confidence is tied to their role as mother. While the broader political goals of changing society, schools and employment opportunities are crucial to ensure that future generations of women have more choice, the pragmatics of working in an area with a particular group are clear. It would be destructive and presumptuous to devalue that area of pride, if there is nothing else to offer. Ironically, this is precisely what the 'deficit' mothering model does. In its fierce attempt to improve possibly shaky situations, women often lose confidence and self-esteem.

While the women I knew at Moorland were often anti-'women's lib' in their expressed viewpoints, they themselves were aware of needing time and space to be with women. They rejected the idea of male staff in the drop-in. While fathers were encouraged to participate in the nursery, no concerted efforts were made to increase their use of the drop-in. As with the all-female consciousness-raising groups of the 1970s, women in the drop-in wanted to establish their own agenda, something they knew that men can disrupt. Practically speaking, topics of birth experience, bottle- or breast-feeding and contraception are much more difficult in a mixed group.

While as a professional I endorse the need for more involvement of fathers and for a more equal sharing of family responsibilities between men and women, it was clearly not what was wanted by the women with whom I was working. I never hid my own views and my own experience of sharing parenting responsibility, but I respected the women's right to reject my opinion.

Anti-sexist practice

Within the nursery, attempts were made to raise awareness through book selection, toy choice, dressing-up clothes, etc. Children can be directly challenged in their assumptions about sex roles, and it is particularly important to involve men in the nursery in non-traditional roles. However, if parents are to be genuinely involved they must be consulted, and the purpose behind such activities should be made explicit. Parents will bring in books that reflect traditional views, and introduce games, songs and activities that may be sexist in content. One mother at Moorland came in with a book, saying, 'Naomi's going to hate this one.' An open system that encourages parents to play a role must delegate some control, for this ability to share control is fundamental to parental involvement that does not devalue parents.

At Moorland we ran workshops on sex roles and constantly questioned and challenged traditional views. However, the basic relationships between parents and staff were such that the inherent inequality of power was considerably lessened. Value judgements are dangerous only when those making them have power over those being

judged. Where adults are perceived as equals, such judgements are accorded the status of individual opinions. While
I never gave up my right to express my views, I never made
professional judgements based on a parent's willingness to
adopt my politics.

As with all democratic institutions, the vocal will of the
majority could not trample on the rights of the minority. In
this respect the centre does not tolerate racism. A decision
to exclude black mothers is unacceptable. A decision to
accept as legitimate a woman's belief that the best thing for
children is to have a mother at home is acceptable. The
difference is that the mother's view affects her decision
only and does not prevent others from making different
choices. By definition a system that respects individuals cannot support or implement racist views held by
individuals.

There is a sad assumption about working with parents
that presumes an adversarial relationship. Somehow
people believe that if you relinquish power to non-
professionals they will make ridiculous demands that
openly conflict with professional philosophy. In my experience this was not the case. Differences of opinion were
based on well-considered judgements on both sides. The
principle of non-professionals having ultimate control over
statutory agencies is established in local-government structures; officers of local-authority services are answerable to
county council members. Sadly, it is often not the case that
those members represent the client groups who require the
services.

Conclusions

Moorland is one example of parental involvement that is
inherently feminist. It is not presented here as a model to be
replicated. Its strength lies in its responsiveness to the local
community. Other communities have different needs; services that start with consumer demands must be flexible
and responsive to those needs. There are, however, some

general principles that can be applied as a measure of good practice.

Involvement does not aim to make adults better parents, but to make services better tailored to their users, adults as well as children. This involves a major redefinition of professional roles in services for under-fives. Such changes would require that:

- Both staff and parents are clear about the parameters of user control; which issues are genuinely negotiable, and which are not.
- Staff are honestly willing and able to share decision-making and to carry out all decisions, even those they may have opposed.
- Parents involved in management have a clear idea of the initial aims of the service, and those aims must be negotiable once the service is running and users are involved.
- All parents can be involved, but the style of that involvement will depend on the circumstances and willingness of individual parents, and those circumstances will change over the length of time that a family uses the service (Eisenstadt 1983).

The feminist argument in favour of involving parents is valid only for schemes of parental involvement that give mothers some share of control and power. Involvement can be a means for personal growth and an enhancement of self-esteem. It provides women with a base for mutual support and ensures that service providers are sensitive to the needs of adults as well as those of children.

This style of parental involvement can be a difficult and stressful way to run services. One is continually faced with personal and professional conflicts that require compromise and negotiation. For the workers the personal rewards of rich relationships with mothers in a relaxed environment of mutual support are enormous. While feminist ideology extols the rich support that women can offer each other, in the work setting we are often unwilling to acknowledge that such support comes from, as well as goes to, the women who use the services.

CHAPTER 7

'Hallo, Miss Scatterbrain. Hallo, Mr Strong': assessing attitudes and behaviour in the nursery

GLEN THOMAS

Research indicates that sexual inequalities are inherent in our education system (Whyte 1983, p. 5). However, this research has largely been conducted in secondary schools, and it is perhaps because of the emphasis on academic achievement, subject choice and career options that primary teachers have displayed a reluctance to acknowledge their role in the shaping of sex-stereotyped behaviour. Undoubtedly much of the learning of sex roles occurs within the family and through the media, but the early years of schooling also have long-term effects. The outcome of learning experiences that occur during this period must contribute to the fact that girls 'do well academically but, in the long run, to less ambitious effect in their careers' (ILEA 1982, p. 26).

It is during the primary years of schooling that girls begin the process of 'learning to lose' (Spender and Sarah 1980) – not simply from the explicit curriculum but from the messages they receive from the 'hidden' curriculum, which includes school organization, books and resources, language, playground facilities, assemblies, extra-curricular activities and above all the attitudes and expectations of the staff. Judith Whyte argues that education in primary schools is unduly geared towards boys' interests, and maintains that they receive more teacher time and attention than girls (1983, p. 11). Katherine Clarricoates's research revealed that teachers in the early years of schooling classify children according to their sex and expect sex-stereotyped behaviour from them (Clarricoates 1980, pp. 26–41), a factor that tends to heighten rather than diminish the differences between the sexes.

This chapter describes an attempt I made during one academic year to investigate the extent to which these stereotyped attitudes towards sex roles were held by the children and staff in two nursery classes of an inner-city primary school. The following account matches the pattern of the study, which began with personal observations and went on to involve nursery staff in the monitoring of children's play preferences by means of tick-lists. The results of these lists were then discussed with the staff, and I also attempted to discover the teachers' feelings about sexism in general. One of the main questions raised in the discussions related to the amount of time staff allocated to girls and boys, and I then analysed my own practice with this in mind. Finally I discussed the issue with parents, in an attempt to determine whether or not staff were justified in their assertion that sexism in children is mainly a result of influences at home.

My reasons for attempting such a study relate to the fact that although in theory there may appear to be recognition of the need to eliminate sexism in primary schools, in practice it occurs only at an extremely superficial level, if at all. Fundamental attitudes remain unchanged; school staff refuse to acknowledge their own sexism or, if they do, fail to recognize it as a problem and thus maintain the status quo.

As a teacher attempting to change the sexist attitudes and actions that reveal themselves in my *own* behaviour and language, I hoped that any questions raised by my observations could be used as a basis for discussion with colleagues on the issue of sex-role stereotyping, and that we could work together towards the development of an anti-sexist school policy. The study, which in its entirety involved both nursery and infant classes, was not intended to be quantitative, and the resulting evidence was in fact insufficient to formulate generalizable statements about sex-role stereotyping. It nevertheless raised questions that have implications for the way we operate in the early years of schooling.

First impressions

On my initial visits to the nursery, conversations with staff revealed a belief that sex stereotyping occurred either at home or 'when they get higher up the school' and that for their part staff endeavoured to 'treat them all the same'. As far as the activities provided were concerned, nursery staff considered they were used 'equally' by both sexes.[1]

However, from casual observations my perception of the situation did not correspond with that of the staff. It appeared to me that the girls generally occupied themselves in a quieter fashion and were 'better behaved' than the boys. Whilst the girls frequently played in the home corner, boys seemed to prefer activities using big bricks and constructional toys. The girls did not use the outside area as often as the boys, especially the climbing frame, and there was little evidence of cross-sex play, either in the classrooms or out of doors.

I began a closer observation of the situation by focusing on the home corner, where from experience I expected to find most evidence of stereotypical behaviour. During the first session, apart from a group of boys who rushed in and out again immediately, only one boy used this area together with five girls. The girls busied themselves pretending to be 'mummies cooking the dinner' and seemed prepared to allow the boy to participate in their role-play because of his quiet passivity. On another occasion four girls and a rather quiet boy took turns to manipulate a puppet behind a model television screen. During their play they were twice interrupted by several boys who attempted to break up the performance by overturning chairs, kicking, fighting with each other, snatching the puppet and throwing it to the floor. On the third visit I listened to the conversations of children as they dressed dolls in the home corner, and it was apparent that they had a very definite idea of what constitutes sex-appropriate clothing.

My observations in the home corner confirmed the impression I had gained on earlier visits, that girls *did* predominate in this area and engaged in domestic 'mothering' activities and in so doing they reinforced sex stereotypes. The majority of boys who visited the home corner came to disrupt activities. Their behaviour matched Whyte's description of boys 'making raids' on the wendy house and threatening those playing there (1983, p. 31).

Involving the staff

Rather than simply discuss with the nursery staff the questions raised by my observations, it seemed more valuable at this stage to involve them in observing the behaviour of girls and boys. The children were allowed to move around both classrooms, playground and garden area, choosing from a range of activities. A simple method of monitoring was required to discover whether or not their play preferences revealed any patterns of behaviour that were sex related. Although not all the staff were convinced of the need to tackle sexism in the early years they were willing to be involved in these observations, and one of them suggested tick-lists.

Together we designed the lists to include all the available activities and involve all nursery staff (see Figure 7.1). It was originally intended that they should be checked at thirty-minute intervals, but this proved impractical as staff, for various reasons, were unable to tick them at the prescribed times. It was agreed that a sheet bearing the children's names should be kept for each classroom and outside area and ticked at random intervals throughout the day, at the convenience of the staff, rather than at timed

Boy C	Boy B	Boy A	Girl C	Girl B	Girl A			
						Sand		
						Water		
						Book corner		
						Home corner		
						Music corner		
						Painting	CREATIVE	
						Collage		
						Drawing		
						Other		
						Plasticine	PLIABLE	
						Play-dough		
						Clay		INDOOR ACTIVITIES
						Other		
						Lego	CONSTRUCTIONAL	
						Sticklebricks		
						Building bricks		
						Large bricks		
						Other		
						Sewing	MANIPULATIVE	
						Weaving		
						Other		
						Dressing-up	IMAGINATIVE	
						Puppets		
						Maths game	MISCELLANEOUS	
						Puzzles		
						Bicycles		
						Prams		
						Trolleys		
						Wheelbarrows		
						Scooters		OUTDOOR ACTIVITIES
						Milk crates		
						Barrels		
						See-saw		
						Hoops		
						Balls		
						Climbing frames		

FIGURE 7.1 *Tick-list*

intervals. Obviously the results obtained were not statistically significant. However, as they were kept by a number of different people over a period of three weeks and revealed similar patterns of behaviour, they have some validity.

More important than the collection of scientific data was the fact that staff were involved in observing what was happening in the nursery and were therefore more likely to become aware of any sex-stereotyped behaviour. An increased awareness does not necessarily guarantee a change in attitudes and behaviour, but it is certainly a step towards it.

Figure 7.1 is a suggested plan for a tick-list, which in a modified form could provide staff with useful information about the behaviour of children in their charge. One such modification could be to concentrate on only one or two activities each week rather than the entire range simultaneously. Additionally the list could be modified to provide staff with an opportunity to record the way children used the various activities and whether or not their behaviour was consistent throughout, e.g. how girls behave in the playground area in comparison with the way they behave in the home corner. Where more than one member of staff is involved in making observations it is essential to spend time discussing and defining terms.

The main points revealed by the observations made by nursery staff at random intervals over a period of three weeks are described below. In addition I have included the opinions of the staff, which emerged during our subsequent discussion.

The teachers were not in total agreement with the findings, although they were not altogether surprised by them. When reminded of their original statement that all children used all activities equally they attributed this to the fact that in previous years there had been more boys than girls on roll and they felt this imbalance had to some extent masked the preferences displayed by the different sexes. Involvement in this type of classroom monitoring had made staff realize that all the children were capable of

longer periods of concentration than they had previously
believed possible; they were now more aware of the
activities preferred by both sexes, although not all the
areas monitored by the tick-lists revealed significant
differences.

Our discussion of the findings was extremely valuable in
that it raised a number of questions that have direct implications for education, which we later used to formulate
some ideas for good practice.

Discoveries and discussions

Indoor Activities

> More girls than boys used the home corner,
> and girls used it more repeatedly than the
> boys.

The staff asserted that this was a hangover from the past
when a great deal of unnecessary divisions by gender were
made. Children had formerly to ask permission to use the
home corner, and girls, because they were considered more
likely to use it quietly, were allowed to use it more often
than boys. Despite attempts of newer staff to change the
ethos in the nursery, certain old attitudes still prevailed,
especially amongst older and less flexible staff. However, I
felt that positive efforts needed to be made to encourage
girls to move out of the home corner, which appears to
reinforce stereotyped behaviour. If girls practise only
'housework and child care' then their opportunities to
experience other activities will be limited. Boys need to be
encouraged to use the home corner more often and in a
less disruptive way and to realize that it is acceptable for
them to be involved in 'caring' roles. If we ensure that
this occurs then there is a greater possibility that boys
will be able to openly express the range of emotions they
feel.

> More girls than boys used the pliable materials, which include clay, plasticine and play-dough.

The staff maintained that an activity like play-dough plus rollers and cutters was more likely to be used by the girls, whereas a 'messy' activity like clay or compost mixed with water was less likely. This could be related to the way in which female staff present such 'messy' activities to the girls, because often they find it difficult to conceal their own dislike of such play. So long as girls believe they shouldn't get dirty it precludes the possibility of engaging in a wide range of experiences.

> More boys than girls used constructional toys, and boys used them more repeatedly than girls.

The boys' greater use of constructional toys was not regarded as typical, as the staff considered that their use varied enormously depending on the type of constructional play available. However, boys were more likely to construct cars, planes and guns, which they would incorporate into imaginative play. Probably the fact that girls are not exposed to constructional toys in their pre-nursery years to the same extent as boys tends to make them less confident and skilful in their use. If we believe that early experience of constructional play is a factor in determining a person's confidence in the use of scientific and technological ideas and equipment, then we need to ensure that all children's attempts are praised, *especially* the girls', who may lack experience.

> More boys than girls were involved in imaginative activities.

It was felt that there were certain aspects of imaginative play that involved both sexes equally, such as play-people and puppets. However, staff should be aware of the fact that these toys are often used in very different ways, with girls 'putting baby to bed' and boys playing 'chase' games with toy cars and planes.

> More girls than boys were involved in manipulative activities that require fine motor control, e.g. sewing, and fine interlocking pieces such as figure-craft.

Staff believed, contrary to the evidence of the tick-lists, that boys used these activities more than girls. Their disagreement suggests that check-lists of this nature can be extremely useful in bringing the fact to one's attention that behaviours may not be exactly as one imagines. Such information should naturally inform future approaches.

Outdoor Activities

> More boys than girls used the bicycles, and boys used them more often than girls.

Staff agreed that boys did dominate playground activities, especially the bicycles, which they 'saved' for each other. This was attributed to the particular type of boys present in the nursery at this time, who were always keen to play outside.

> Prams were used more often by girls than by boys.

When boys were observed using prams, their use was described as 'wheelbarrows', whereas girls were seen to be 'caring'. Perhaps this description reflects the staff's stereotyped views.

> Boys used the balls more than girls did.

There was agreement that the boys played with the balls more than the girls did, especially the footballs, which were rarely used for cross-sex play. Again, this was attributed to the nature of the particular group of boys. As boys seemed to dominate the outside space and activities, I felt we needed to discuss how we could encourage girls to use them more often, since they need the same opportunities as boys to be active and adventurous through physical exercise and spatial exploration.

Naturally, monitoring children's behaviour in this way required extra effort on the part of staff but as it resulted in a heightened awareness of stereotyped behaviour it seemed worthwhile. Such awareness should enable us to operate so that all children develop as 'highly individual people in their own right' (Byrne 1978, p. 16).

Talking to staff

It is understandable that many staff find an examination of their own attitudes and behaviour more 'threatening' than observations of children's behaviour. However, because this appears to be a crucial step in effecting any kind of change, I decided after using the tick-lists that loosely structured interviews would allow discussion of the issue of sex-role stereotyping and enable me to determine to some extent the attitudes held by the nursery staff.

The staff, who were all female, agreed that it was important that both sexes should be given equal opportunities in school. With one exception they believed that they had not been afforded the same opportunities in life as boys, because either brothers had been 'favoured' or facilities such as science laboratories and woodwork equipment had been lacking at single-sex schools. Only one member of staff expected different behaviour from the sexes, expecting girls to behave 'nicely' and boys to be 'rough but not bad'. The remainder considered that although they didn't necessarily expect different behaviour, parental and societal attitudes encouraged it.

Despite the fact that they all tried to treat children as individuals and not according to their sex, they admitted to not always being successful. Only one teacher seemed fully aware of how subtle this differential behaviour could be and attributed her awareness to recent attendance on in-service Training courses concerned with the subject of sexism in the nursery environment.

Several of the staff were surprised by the information that girls achieved slightly better than boys in examinations up to O-level. They regarded poor career guidance as the reason why girls did not usually choose subjects to enhance their job prospects. Only one of them believed that expectations and attitudes held by staff involved in the early years of schooling could be influential in shaping these subject and career choices.

The nursery staff all believed that boys should be 'as gentle as girls and girls as tough as a boy can be' but considered that whilst society might be prepared to accept 'bossy' girls it was much harder for 'cissy' boys to be accepted. They were uncertain of the amount of time and attention they gave to each sex but felt it was unlikely that they gave more to boys. It was suggested that this was much more likely to be the case in the infant and junior departments where more direction of activities occurs.

From these discussions with the staff, further questions were raised, which were also used to develop ideas for good practice. One important question related to the way in which teacher time and attention are divided between the sexes and resulted in my own use of the GIST (Girls into Science and Technology) Classroom Observation Schedule.[2]

Classroom Observation Schedule

Although I believe it to be extremely valuable to monitor the behaviour of children, if one seriously wishes to alter one's own attitudes and behaviour then it is essential to monitor and evaluate this in the classroom. I began to monitor my own practice by means of the GIST Classroom Observation Schedule, modified for nursery and infant classrooms. This schedule enables staff to discover how they share their time between the sexes by, for example, counting the number of times they ask questions of both sexes or how many times each sex comments spontaneously.

The observations were conducted in two lower infant classes but it seems appropriate to mention them here as the process of assessment can just as easily be carried out in a nursery. A colleague and I watched each other work and then agreed to arrange another of these reciprocal sessions on a future occasion. We considered that, although the results were insufficient to reach firm conclusions, they would provide a useful input at a staff meeting and, we hoped, encourage colleagues to participate in this kind of critical evaluation of their own practice. Using this schedule reminded me that repeated assessment of one's practice is essential, and that the schedule, if operated reciprocally with a colleague, is an ideal instrument for building mutual trust.

Talking to parents

Parents have an enormous influence on the shaping of sex roles, which are already well established by the time children arrive at nursery school. If children do bring these sex-stereotyped attitudes it is easy for teachers to ignore the role of the school in reinforcing them. It is easier to blame parents than to recognize that one's own behaviour and the school organization are contributory factors. It would appear to be more beneficial to initiate a dialogue between parents and school, rather than apportion blame, so I decided to interview a number of the nursery children's parents in an attempt to discover if they considered that children of different sexes should be treated differently and encouraged to behave in a manner 'appropriate' for their sex.

Of the six parents I interviewed, four were women. Since it is usually mothers who collect their children from the nursery school it was more difficult to make contact with fathers. The interviews, which were loosely structured, were tape-recorded, as this enabled us to chat informally rather than me take notes and make parents feel they were being interrogated.

Both men believed that it was a better life for a man. Whilst the women all said that they were happy being women, all but one, who had been encouraged to continue her education, considered that they had not received the same opportunities as the males in their family when leaving school:

> When I wanted to do a hairdressing apprentice with no money, they wouldn't let me 'cos I was only going to get married, but he was encouraged to become an apprentice electrician, even though he didn't earn any money.

Everyone was in agreement that women and men should be given equal opportunities in life. However, when we discussed the career choices open to both sexes, it appeared they were unconvinced that 'equality' could be a reality. Although it was felt that

> as long as they're able then they should do whatever they want, even if they want to drive those big articulated lorries . . .

doubts were expressed about the possibility of this:

> the only drawback is that we have to have children. . . . But I think our build prevents us. I mean I can't imagine a woman humping a great big bin around.

According to the men there were differences that might prevent complete equality. One attributed it to physique and the other to intellect:

> she's too slow . . . I think it's because of her gender. She's . . . slow, so I said okay let's try for a man . . . then we

realized that when we had that man he was so quick in doing things. . . . I think maybe because she's a woman she's slow.

All the parents considered they tried to treat their daughters or sons in the same way and felt it was important for them to be encouraged to participate equally in household chores. However, when discussed at greater length it became clear that they did differentiate in their treatment of the sexes. Despite the fact that all except one male agreed that boys should be allowed to play with dolls, and girls to play with cars and planes, etc., only one woman had bought a doll specifically for her son. They all said that when faced with buying presents for children of friends and family they would buy only sex-appropriate toys. Action Man was greatly approved of as it had in some way made the notion of boys playing with dolls acceptable, but the aggressive nature of this doll appeared to have been overlooked. Only one parent insisted he would not allow his son to have a doll or any other toys he considered inappropriate for his sex: 'I always say, that's for a girl, because he knows anyway what is for boys and girls.'

When we discussed the subject of clothes it became apparent that attitudes about appropriate clothing for the sexes were still relatively traditional. The women appeared to favour feminine clothes for girls; while they considered it acceptable for girls to wear jeans, it was not totally right for boys to wear pink because 'it's that cissy thing again, isn't it?' or, as another parent said, 'It's just the way . . . the attitude of the world again.' Whilst one father was concerned to dress his children in practical clothes, the other insisted he would never allow his son to wear anything 'feminine'.

When we discussed the kind of emotional behaviour they considered appropriate for either sex, it was interesting that none of them chose to discuss this in relation to their daughters, but they considered it immediately in relation to boys. The women were in total agreement about the need for boys and men to be encouraged to 'show their feelings' and 'have the outlet to cry'. One of the men said he did not

like to see people of either sex cry, but the other wished his
son was less aggressive and more sensitive, like himself:

> I've always been more sensitive than many other males,
> especially in my family. . . . I've always been quiet and
> enjoyed reading, whereas he seems to enjoy more boyish
> activities, fighting particularly.

Probably the greatest advances towards equality have
been made in respect of housework, child care and especially cooking, and the comments of male and female
parents reflected this. However, given that changes have
occurred, there was still the underlying assumption that
these areas are nevertheless the province of women. Where
husbands did participate in housework, cooking and child
care, none of them assumed responsibility for all the domestic chores. Even in one family where the husband was
unemployed, although he was prepared to collect the
children from school and do the cooking, he was not willing
to be involved in housework. His wife considered it was her
role to work full-time and do the housework – 'It's the law;
we're made to fit in.'

When husbands did assume these roles, on occasions
when their wives were working or sick, the women felt that
they were fortunate or had 'a lucky one'. Whilst one man
had undertaken the entire responsibility for the home and
children because his wife worked while he studied, the
other shared responsibility for the chores with his wife
despite a certain reluctance: 'I know it's her job in a
way. . . . I said to myself it's her job, but we have to help
each other.'

Overall there was a definite feeling that things had
changed and women were given more equality of opportunity than in the past. What parents did not appear to be
fully aware of, however, were the career choices that are in
theory available to both sexes. They tended to consider the
issue in terms of physique. They were unaware of the
evidence suggesting that women are capable of great
endurance; that there are greater differences in strength
within the sexes than between them; and that women's

gynaecological make-up does not necessarily restrict their involvement in physical exercise (ILEA 1984). Only one parent clung to the notion that women were less intelligent than men.

In relation to the differential treatment of children the parents had somewhat ambivalent attitudes. While on one level they considered it important to treat both sexes in the same way and offer them similar experiences, on another level they were heavily influenced by societal attitudes and expectations. This was apparent in relation to the type of toys considered appropriate, the clothes worn and the emotional behaviour considered suitable for each sex. For although they believed that boys should be encouraged to be more 'caring' and sensitive, there was recognition that society does not regard these traits as admirable in a man.

Whilst advances have been made in relation to domestic responsibilities, and women today make more demands on their partners, these advances often obscure the fundamental attitudes that nevertheless exist about women's role in society. However, this does not alter the fact that we as teachers should avoid making assumptions about the behaviour and attitudes of parents. We must recognize that all parents want more equal opportunities for their children even if they are uncertain how they might be obtained. More important, just as many teachers are, they are attempting to make changes in their lives, however unsuccessful they may be, and in certain areas have already succeeded.

The immediate question to arise from this, which we as teachers must consider if we wish to work alongside parents in an attempt to counter the influences of society, is: how can a home–school dialogue best be promoted?

Towards an anti-sexist policy

An investigation of this kind is useful in the formulation of a school anti-sexist policy. When questions are raised by such observations they can be used to promote discussion on the

issue of sexism in school and to heighten teachers' awareness of the need to consider the issue seriously. There are
other aspects of the school and its organization that will
need investigation when developing a school policy, including language, books and resources, visual images,
staffing and in-service training. A change in teachers' attitudes and behaviour or the development of such a policy
will not necessarily overcome stereotyping, since schools
are only part of the wider society. However, we must not
use this as an excuse for apathy – 'countering sexism is part
of the struggle to extend choices and opportunities for
everyone' (Stones 1983).

Notes

The title of this chapter is borrowed from *Little Miss Scatterbrain* by
Roger Hargreaves (1981).

1. The term 'equally' was used in a very loose way, and staff did not
   make clear whether it meant that girls and boys engaged in an activity
   in the same way or for similar periods of time.
2. GIST Classroom Observation Schedule obtainable from Girls into
   Science and Technology, Manchester Polytechnic, 9a Didsbury Park,
   Manchester M20 0LH.

CHAPTER 8

Unclouded minds saw unclouded visions: visual images in the nursery

NAIMA BROWNE AND PAULINE FRANCE

In our work with young children we have become increasingly aware of just how much they notice differences between people and how perceptive they are about the way people are depicted. In our contact with other nursery staff we found that many adults were unwilling to take this into account when choosing new resources and reviewing existing ones. Yet upon undertaking such a review, staff have been surprised to discover the extent of stereotyping.

Nursery staff also have an ambivalent attitude towards discussion with children about differences between people. They encourage children to talk about their personal experiences, and to learn from the observation, comparison and classification of differences. Yet when children put these two aspects of learning together and try to make sense out of observable differences between people and those that are socially constructed, staff tend to avoid being drawn into serious discussion. It is common to hear under-fives workers assert that young children cannot be sexist, racist or otherwise discriminatory. However, young children are certainly capable of being hurt by sexist and racist discrimination; to deny that this happens in nursery establishments not only is naïve, but also serves to condone sexist and racist practice.

To support our own work and encourage colleagues to develop anti-sexist and anti-racist policy and practice we set out to review and evaluate recently published nursery resources and to suggest strategies for producing more positive material and for talking about the images on offer in the nursery. In this chapter we firstly argue for the importance of providing resources that accurately and sensitively reflect the diversity in children's lives. Then we give a more detailed description of the review of resources that we undertook. Thirdly we offer strategies for extending, adapting or replacing visual material to ensure the provision of more positive images.

Handling diversity with young children

'We treat them all the same'
The comment that all children are treated equally crops up with monotonous regularity in discussions with nursery staff about anti-sexist and anti-racist approaches to learning and materials. The assumption seems to be that nothing needs to be changed, since all children are receiving an equal education. Indeed it could be argued that if all children do receive the same treatment from adults who are working to a clearly defined anti-sexist and anti-racist policy then things *will* be moving in a positive direction. Sadly this is not always the case.

Differentiated and unequal treatment begins for children growing up in this society at birth, if not before (a point discussed in Chapter 4). The myth of 'opposite sexes' is upheld, justified and manifested in how children are treated and in what behaviour is expected from them. They are encouraged to believe that sex differences are not just anatomical but are associated with behaviour, interests and skills. Sex-stereotyped attitudes and ideas are transmitted to children in three main ways – through language, through non-verbal actions and behaviour and through visual images – and this has been shown to go on even in those classrooms where staff assert that they treat all children the same (Serbin 1978, Clarricoates 1980).

Given this prevailing habit of differentiating between girls and boys even before they start in school, it is too simplistic of staff to assert that there are no differences between the boys and girls in their charge and that by giving them the same treatment they are being actively anti-sexist. The differences between the boys and girls revolve upon the different experiences they have to bring to the institution; to be truly anti-sexist, staff need to consider how they can help each child broaden her or his experiences and develop their full potential, without either a sense of inferiority (all too commonly found in girls even at an early age) or a sense of superiority (the type of feeling that enables boys to take over activities and toys, demand all the adult's attention and claim all the floor space) (Belotti 1975). To achieve this is to move beyond the 'equal treatment' approach.

The multilingual nursery can be a rich and stimulating environment if the diverse experiences of all children are fully recognized and given equal status and freedom to develop. To deny or seek to eradicate differences between children (physical, linguistic, cultural, religious) is to deny individuality and subscribe to a 'melting-pot' assimilationist ideology. This approach has prevailed for too long in schools as a response to the presence of ethnic-minority children and results in children being treated as though they all have the same background – that of 'white Anglo-Saxon Protestants' (Racism in schools 1981).

From our experience it seems that the philosophy of treating children all the same, no matter how well intentioned, serves to blur several issues:

1 Differences between children – often socially created differences – do exist in the nursery; for example, the relative status between boys and girls. These become evident if we spend time and observe who each child

plays with, which toys and activities are selected and what type of play is developed.

2 In the light of this fact, can we really be sure that 'equal treatment' is truly neutral and not influenced by our own cultural background and gender-associated expectations? In reality are we not providing a learning curriculum that favours white boys?

3 Do we consider the 'hidden' curriculum and how that reflects our equal treatment? For example, the amount of adult attention, day-to-day organization and grouping of children and the type of reception we give parents.

4 How does a policy of equal treatment help us to recognize and support the differences that develop between individuals of the same sex and cultural group?

5 How can equal treatment equip children to cope in an unequal society where some groups are made to feel inferior from an early age?

6 Given the strong educational justification for helping children to notice, talk about and classify difference – the stock-in-trade of early mathematical tasks – why do we avoid or feel uncomfortable about discussing differences between people?

7 Is the equal treatment approach not merely a cover-up for a reluctance to counter the over-generalized differences prevalent in sex and race stereotyping and for a similar reluctance to adopt an anti-sexist, anti-racist approach, which is considered to be too political?

When turning our attention towards the learning resources needed to complement an anti-sexist and anti-racist approach we realized that we needed to find images that accurately reflect diversity amongst people.

'Young Children Don't Notice Difference'
The comment that young children are unaware of differences between people is frequently used to justify the rejection of any attempts to discuss and reflect diversity with them. Generally it is coupled with a wish to preserve the status quo, where girls and women, ethnic minorities

and the working class are stereotyped and under-represented in learning materials.

In claiming that children do not notice such differences, adults are also denying that young children are capable of negative behaviour towards others based solely on physical differences. When children's derogatory reactions towards skin colour differences are ignored,

> such behaviour may reinforce racism. For instance a white child may object to sitting next to another child because of that child's race. The teacher may ignore the statement or say only, 'don't say that, it's not nice'. If nothing is to be done to re-establish the self-esteem of the child of colour and to change the white child's behaviour – that's not just avoiding the issue, it's racism.
>
> (Wilson *et al.* 1980)

On the issue of noticing and talking about gender differences, the situation is in many ways more complex. Children are trained to expect differences between males and females – differences not only in terms of physical appearance and abilities but those that operate on a cognitive, emotional and interest level too. Such differences are socially created as extreme opposites and are over-generalized; for instance, all boys are expected to be tough, strong and independent, whilst all girls should be in need of protection and dependent. No leeway is allowed for the probability that there will be diversity between people of the same sex or that there is similarity between males and females. In addition most young children are nurtured into the 'girls can't do . . .' whilst 'boys wouldn't want to . . .' line of thinking.

Although it is commonly denied that young children can perceive outwardly apparent physical differences – such as skin colour, size, age and physical ability – they are expected to handle the subtleties of what the labels 'male' and 'female' denote as a matter of course. An awareness of difference between the sexes does not develop in young children simply because that difference is there in the first place. It is nurtured by what children learn to be socially acceptable in their daily lives, and in the two-dimensional images of males and females that surround them at home and outside, as well as in the toys they are given to play with (Belotti 1975, Wilson *et al.* 1980).

Research evidence, and our own work with under-fives, has shown that children do start to notice physical differences between people and learn to apply labels that create divisions between members of our society. Although, as Troyna (1983) points out, much research on the self-image of black children has been questioned (mostly for false conclusions drawn by researchers and for their failure to consider the impact made by images in our society), it is possible to conclude that

> differential and evaluative attitudes towards race are prevalent in all children at an earlier age than most parents and teachers care to admit. Colour blind approaches are not only inappropriate but also dangerous because they allow racist attitudes to develop unchallenged.
>
> (Troyna 1983)

In the United States, Mary Ellen Goodman worked with one hundred black and white children aged between 3 and 5 years. She found that

> racial awareness was present and that twenty-five per cent of the children were expressing strongly entrenched race-related values by the age of four.
>
> (Wilson *et al.* 1980)

The tendency for young girls to have limited expectations of the roles females can play has also been documented by people working in nurseries. It has been attributed to the images that they see in society at large, as well as to the way they are personally treated. Sometimes these images prove more powerful than the reality of the children's own lives; for instance, a friend found that her four-year-old daughter adamantly believed that women cannot be doctors despite the fact that her own doctor was a woman. This kind of assertion can easily be countered with positive learning resources – where they exist. Such resources can help girls become more confident about themselves and their relationship to others, and are something boys too can benefit from:

> hearing stories about working mothers caused kindergarten girls to increase the number and type of job they thought were appropriate for women.
>
> (Campbell and Wirtenberg 1978)

By presenting girls and boys with positive images of female characters McArthur and Eisen found that children were more likely to view girls as achievement oriented. They concluded:

> If one wishes to promote more equal representation of men and women in achieving roles in our society, a change in the representation of females in children's books may be a useful step forward. . . . it does not seem unreasonable to expect that young girls' prolonged exposure to stereotypic children's books may contribute to their lower level of adult achievement.
>
> (1976)

In an article on sex stereotyping and toys, Dr Renée Queen points out that the toy market has been slow in responding to demands for change in the representation of females, especially in the type of packaging and promotion of products employed. Yet she has found that

> children respond to messages about genderised toys from a myriad of sources . . . these cues become deterrents to play by age three.
>
> (1978)

It is thus important to consider the type of images we promote in the learning materials that we give to young children. Not only this; we need also to review all resources to estimate the range and balance of images. We must reflect on our role in presenting such material and monitor carefully how children respond to it. Advocates of an approach that treats all children the same tend to assume that there should simply be an equal balance of images – for instance, the same number of girl main characters as boy main characters in a story. Although this is not adequate for

an anti-sexist approach, it is interesting to find how provocative even such moderate steps in this direction can be.

If we are to treat all children equally well, then we must
not treat them as though they are all the same. To counter
the negative discrimination and differentiation that prevail
in society, we must take positive steps in favour of certain
groups and radically change the images we provide. As
Gaby Weiner points out in criticizing equal opportunities
approaches.

> policies of equal opportunities have attempted to resolve
> the situation by trying to educate girls, ethnic minorities,
> working-class and handicapped pupils to fit the white
> middle-class able-bodied male model. If the fit is faulty,
> blame is put on individual pupils rather than on the inad-
> equacy of the schooling.
>
> (1985)

In addition to reviewing and evaluating learning resources one by one in our survey, we needed to take into
account the following general considerations:

(1) The balance of images that are presented to a group of
children: this meant not only deciding upon the individual
effect of learning equipment but also assessing the collective effect of all the resources on offer in a classroom. We
found that sometimes images seem relatively innocuous in
their own right, yet once put alongside other images they
take on a new dimension. For example, a poster showing a
young girl carefully stepping over a puddle is harmless
enough until we find that other posters, on the same theme
of rain, all show boys splashing, stamping, jumping and
having an enjoyable active time. The overall impression
given is that girls are careful about their appearance and are
unable to enjoy themselves, whereas boys are carefree and
know how to enjoy themselves.

(2) Related to this point is the distinction we needed to
keep in our minds between offensive, caricatured and
stereotyped images that remain just this no matter what
situation they appear in, and images that reflect one aspect
of people's lives or habits or nature. The latter become

offensive only if they are the sole image used to depict a certain group of people.

For example, caricatured images of females – witches, fat ladies, sex objects, evil stepmothers – are offensive wherever and whenever they occur, whereas the image of a woman or girl in a caring, servicing role is in itself inoffensive. We recognize, after all, that a large proportion of women and girls engage in caring and servicing tasks at some time in their lives. Yet if these are the *only* noncaricatured images of females on offer to young children then they will present a depressingly limited view of what women can and do achieve.

(3) The match, or more frequently mismatch, between the visual image and accompanying text or spoken word needs to be considered. For example, we found several instances where the positive intention of the text in a book has been ruined by stereotyped images incorporated into the illustrations. In some cases these are subtle points cropping up in detailed illustrations, but sometimes they are extremely obvious. The importance of the visual clues, over the spoken ones, to the development of a story is considerable – particularly with children new to the language being used, who will be searching the illustrations to gain insights into the story content. Children are likely to get totally different messages at times, if their attention is simply focused on the illustrations:

> The visual material constructs levels of meaning not present in the text. . . . So while a written sentence may carry a conversation between mother and child about a toy, the accompanying image in placing the two in the kitchen or bedroom rather than in the garage working on the car may represent the norm, but it also privileges the norm and establishes the boundary within which the mother–child relation is constructed for the reader.
>
> (Goodall 1981)

Equally, the positive effect of non-stereotyped images in visual material can be undermined by the way it is presented and talked about, or ignored. For instance, the value of a picture story that shows a woman cutting wood to extend the legs on her son's bed is lost if coupled with the comment, 'Poor woman, she hasn't got a man to do it.'

(4) We need to consider any type of learning resource in the light of how it is packaged, presented and promoted. Children take notice of the pictures and photographs used not only on toy boxes and packages, but also on any other sort of learning material. They quickly learn from these just who the resources are intended for.

Children love to look at toy catalogues and magazines and pick up similar messages when they see photographs of other children playing with toys. These messages are even more vividly reinforced by television advertising, which tends to consolidate sex and race stereotypes. Toy shops are prone to group toys according to traditional notions of sex divisions and sometimes will openly label their sections as 'girls' toys' or 'boys' toys'.

Even when toys bear *no* images of people there are subtle ways in which they are sex-stereotyped; for example, by the way they are named: 'handy-*man* tools', 'little *miss* vacuum-cleaner', 'little *doctor*' to contrast with 'little *nurse*' medical kit, and so on.

Evaluation of visual images

With these points in mind we carried out a mini-survey of posters and pictures published between 1979 and 1985 by a journal used by many nursery workers. We found:

1 Nearly twice as many featured males only as opposed to females only.
2 Children were sex-stereotyped in terms of behaviour, activity, role and appearance.
3 Black women and girls were misrepresented, and some ethnic groups were totally absent.
4 Families shown conformed to narrow stereotypes.
5 Fantasy characters perpetuated sexist and racist myths.

We then looked at the images on a range of resources in the nursery including jigsaw puzzles, turn-taking games (e.g. lotto), card games, toy boxes, furnishings, collage and craft materials (e.g. magazines and old greeting cards) and so on. We found that these too tended to show the same characteristics as those listed above.

Books for young children are crammed with pictures and cannot be excluded from any survey of visual images. However, books are not discussed in detail here as there is already a body of published research on sex and race stereotyping in children's books (Dixon 1977a and 1977b, Stones 1983).

Half the World's Population is Female
The high proportion of men and boys featured in posters and pictures is obviously not a true reflection of the world, but seems instead to be an indication of the difference in the relative importance many people in society attribute to females and males. The dominance of males in pictures implicitly suggests to children that men and boys, unlike women and girls, do interesting things worth talking about. This attitude has been a feature of British education, with children being taught about the achievements of men whilst those of women, and particularly of black women, have been undervalued, suppressed or ignored.

This dominance of males is also evident in pictures featuring both females and males. Looking at some of these we got the impression that the women or girls had been added as an afterthought, and they did not appear to play any real part in the scene being depicted. The picture on one photo-puzzle, for example, seems to show a group of girls and boys playing with their bikes and scooters. Closer inspection reveals that in the forefront of the picture are three boys, taking an active interest in the mechanics of their bike, and behind them two girls are standing by, looking uninterested. The 'invisible' female is all too common in resources designed for young children, and, as discussed later, black women are even less visible.

'Look, children, a lady *fireman!'*

If the images surrounding nursery children are to be believed, women do very little apart from caring for their
home and family. The message received by children about
the relative importance of females and males is further
refined by the fact that when women do appear it is often in
a very limited capacity.

In the poster series we analysed, women were shown as
engaging in only twelve different occupations, with the
emphasis on parenting, teaching, nursing and caring for or
servicing others; e.g. shop assistants, school cleaners, sec-
retaries. The majority of women shown were conforming to
stereotyped ideas about 'women's work'. When women
were shown in non-stereotyped occupations, as an ambulance driver and a fire-fighter, it appeared as if the publishers had suffered from a failure of confidence. In the first
case the ambulance driver was shown administering
oxygen to a patient on a stretcher rather than actually driving. In our experience young children have never identified
her as an ambulance driver but have defined her in terms of
her caring role: 'she's making him better' or 'she's putting
him to sleep'. This picture is an ineffective challenge to
the stereotype of the caring woman. In the second case
the picture was a black-and-white photograph on the
reverse of which was a full-colour close-up of a male fire-
fighter. It is not hard to guess which picture most nursery
workers would consider more attractive to children.

Men were shown in almost three times as many different
occupations as women, ranging from farmer to window
cleaner and from doctor to pantomime horse. Women's
employment patterns are still influenced by archaic beliefs
relating to women's 'natural' skills; occupations that are in
some way an extension of domesticity or mothering, e.g.
nursing, cleaning and working with young children, tend
to be associated with women. To present children with
pictures that reflect this merely helps perpetuate the
association.

This narrow sex-stereotyping is a feature of many
puzzles, turn-taking games, books and other learning

materials. There are plenty of photo-puzzles of men at work as train guards, postal workers, doctors and bus drivers. Women are shown as nurses and police officers. In a set of wooden figures all the sailors, astronauts and construction workers are men, whilst women are represented as ballet dancers, airline cabin staff and, inevitably, nurses. Colleagues have argued that the continued use of resources with images such as these is justifiable on the ground that 'it's how things are'. We would argue that it is an unbalanced interpretation of real life. We all know women who are not mothers or who earn their living as scientists, bus drivers, researchers or artists; through not being shown women engaged in as broad a range of activities as men, children begin to think of such women as exceptions. Exceptions, however, tend to prove the rule, as comments such as 'Look, children, a *lady* fireman!' make clear.

The absence of resources depicting men and boys in caring roles gives messages about the acceptability of such roles. Many children have personal experience of being cared for by men, but this is rarely acknowledged. Pictures of men in frilly aprons are not helpful, as they declare that it is a joke for men to wash up or clean the kitchen floor, and furthermore the frills on the apron remind us of who should be doing it!

Children as well as adults are depicted in the pink and blue strait-jackets of socially constructed gender roles. Girls stroke rabbits, whilst boys build dens. Girls in the rain hold umbrellas aloft, whilst boys stamp uninhibitedly in puddles. An 'exceptional' girl plays football with four boys. These images, which variously appeared on posters and puzzles, once more emphasize the delicacy and gentleness expected of girls and the liveliness expected of boys.

Resources that present children with a broad range of images of females and males go some way to encouraging children to see diversity as a fact of life – neither threatening nor unexpected, but something that can be talked about openly and freely.

'Who's in your family?'

There's Mummy and Daddy and a little girl and a little boy. We are white and we live in a semi-detached house with a garden and a garage. Father and son mow the lawn while Mummy and daughter bake cakes in the kitchen.

This image, so beloved of advertisers, is also the most common image of a family presented by nursery resources. It appears in books, on lotto cards and on jigsaw puzzles. A recent survey (The *Observer*, 16th September 1984) found that, despite the fact that only 14 per cent of households in Britain consist of two parents and two or three children, a staggering 79 per cent of adults in the survey believed such a household was typical. If adults with all their experience and analytical skills are still influenced by the images turned out by the media, it is not hard to imagine the effect of such images on a child's understanding of the world.

The reality is very different for many children. There may be one parent present or both; the child may live in a flat or in a maisonette, a caravan or a house; the parents may or may not be of the same cultural background; the parents may be of different ethnic groups. The largest proportion of resources marketed for use in nurseries totally ignores these realities whilst presenting sexist images – mother and daughter doing 'womanly' things whilst fathers and sons get on with the 'manly' things. In this sexist image of a family both females and males are trapped in their stereotyped grooves; the image is also culture-bound in that it presents an idealized image of a white middle-class family. No wonder many nursery workers are turning their hand to producing their own resources and getting very positive feedback from the children.

Sexism and Racism

In the poster series we analysed, black women appeared only four times. It is impossible to reflect the wealth and diversity of black women's experience in four posters. Despite a growing awareness of the need to counter racism in all educational institutions, including nurseries, racist images of women are still being used. An absence of images of women from cultures other than white European is racist and sexist, as it implies that children have nothing to learn from such women. Similarly, images of Asian women only as home-makers, or of black women generally only as bus conductors or nurses, misrepresent black women's experiences and are based on racist and sexist myths about their employment patterns.

To understand why publishers and others continue to fail to provide accurate reflections of real life we need to realize that the visual images each of us regards as appropriate for young children are those that in some way uphold our own values and that we individually see as presenting an accurate reflection of reality. Each of us, however, has a unique perception of 'reality' influenced by our own life experiences and by factors such as gender, race, class and religion. National publishers respond to the demands of their clients, and until very recently there had been a demand only for resources that upheld the dominant, patriarchal, white middle-class, Christian ethos of schools. Publishers therefore would not produce resources that helped challenge the validity of this ethos, so racist images of black women based on white male perceptions were, and unfortunately are still, all too common. Enlightened workers within the publishing field have produced guidelines for themselves and colleagues; but fears that new anti-sexist and anti-racist material will not sell well abroad and is not overwhelmingly demanded by clients in Britain results in publishing houses opting for the conservative approach.

In the same way that some white women are ensuring that children see images reflecting enlightened values in questioning the sexism of white cultures, nursery staff need to ensure that women's values from the broad range of cultures are also reflected in resources presented to young children. Understanding and experience of a culture are necessary if the image presented is to be free from stereotyping and assumptions. Nursery staff must therefore draw on other women's experiences in choosing non-sexist images.

Fantasy Characters

'Humanized' animals run amok in many nurseries and in doing so perpetuate many sexist myths. Illustrators subject animals to the same forms of sexual stereotyping as their human counterparts. Females are depicted as dainty, small and passive with long eyelashes and coy expressions. Males are strong, aggressive, square-jawed and bold. Sex stereotyping in terms of clothing is also a feature of humanized animals. One puzzle we have seen shows a group of animals involved in a race. All the animals competing are male, whilst the females, hampered no doubt by their frilly petticoats, aprons and mop caps, are relegated to the sidelines. Clothes are often the main means of identifying the sex of humanized animals; so females are nearly always dressed in skirts with frills and flounces and frequently have aprons. Males, meanwhile, tend to wear trousers, ties and jackets. Some illustrators have avoided this sex stereotyping. Nancy Carlson's books, for example, feature a dog called Harriet who dresses in dungarees, shorts and on occasions dresses. (1984)

As with images of people, the colours animals wear are significant. Females are dressed in pink and other pastel shades, whilst males wear reds and blues. Such colour coding is not lost on children. In Anthony Browne's book *Willy the Wimp* (1984) a timorous gorilla gains his self-confidence and in doing so appears to become strong and macho; in the process the colour of his keep-fit costume changes from pink to red. A five-year-old said, 'Oh, look, he's a girl, he's got pink on', then pointed to muscle-bound Willy and said, 'But now he's got red one.'

Nursery rhymes and fairy tales are also seen by many to be a necessary part of nursery life. The fact that the majority of rhymes and stories are sexist and racist is not only ignored but is emphasized by the use of pictures and posters that illustrate the stories and songs. Full-colour posters of girls in frilly dresses looking in horror at hairy spiders have a strong visual impact – as do those featuring the Three Bears in which everything belonging to Daddy Bear is much bigger than things belonging to Mummy Bear.

The emphasis on pretty blonde princesses and evil old witches dressed in black provides children with a false set of indications based on conventional myths of beauty and goodness and on the misleading association of darkness, ugliness and evil versus fair skin, beauty and virtue.

What is to be done?

Before being able to develop a set of meaningful criteria with which to assess visual images, nursery workers need to discuss the various issues relating to sexism. They need to understand how it has affected their own and other women's lives and to see how it influences the lives of children. Women also need to learn about the experiences of other women from different cultures. This sharing of experiences takes time and effort but is an essential part of ensuring that anti-sexist images are not racist and that children are presented with images of reality as seen from different viewpoints.

Criteria for evaluating visual images

When evaluating visual material, we need to think about:

1 The character and personality of the females and males: do the images perpetuate or challenge sexist beliefs about 'real men' as strong, independent and assertive and females as dependent, emotional and timid? Are both females and males shown expressing a whole range of emotions?
2 The behaviour and occupations of females and males: are the females home-bound or engaged only in 'women's work' (e.g. cleaning and child care)? Are the males in high-status, interesting occupations requiring skills or physical strength? Are males shown engaged in child care and females in car maintenance?
3 The role of the individuals in relation to others: are females always submissive or present as the male's side-

kick? Are males always dominant decision-makers and problem-solvers?

4 The physical appearance of females and males: does the physical appearance conform to narrow, culturally biased sex stereotypes? Are the females pretty, blonde and slim, neat and well dressed? Are the males muscular and always bigger than the females? Is there the same emphasis on clothes when girls and boys are depicted? Are girls neat and tidy and boys usually not? Are Asian girls ever shown other than with long plaits and *shalwars*? Is there an association between female surface beauty and 'goodness'?

5 The culture and life-style: is there an accurate depiction of a culture or life-style, or is it stereotyped? Are the social relationships between women and men accurately depicted? Is there a concentration on the 'exotic', especially in terms of black women and girls? Are families only ever white middle-class ones consisting of two parents and two children?

6 Other considerations: the relative numbers of females and males and the message this gives; we also try to discover who produced the image, who drew the picture or who took the photograph in order to ascertain whose 'reality' it is.

Groups or individual nursery workers need to construct their own criteria and having done so will need to apply them to a whole range of visual images in the nursery. Books, wall posters, pictures, charts, turn-taking games, card games, puzzles, information signs and instruction cards are all resources that need to be analysed, and perhaps we also need to be aware of the effect of packaging. In addition, materials used for craft and collage activities need to be looked at. Greetings cards, magazines, comics and newspapers are full of sexist and racist stereotypes. Furnishings in a nursery (for example, cushions, curtains and wallpaper) are often culturally biased. Beware of curtains with soldiers, golliwogs, humanized animals and nursery-rhyme characters. The pictures on coat hooks and milk tags can be a source of sex stereotyping, as can the allocation of aprons – for example, flowered ones for girls and striped ones for boys.

It is important to bear in mind the cumulative effect of visual images. The message given by a sexist image in a book may be amplified many times by images in other parts of the nursery.

A fresh approach to classroom resources

Most nurseries are equipped with resources gathered over a number of years and not necessarily chosen by the current staff. With less money available to replace unsuitable resources, workers may find themselves in a dilemma when deciding what to do with those resources judged to be sexist. Whilst some can be modified (e.g. pasting a new picture on top of the offending one on a jigsaw) there remains the problem of what to do with those that cannot. We are aiming to help children learn how to develop an awareness of the issue of sex stereotyping. In addition, children are bombarded daily with sexist images beyond the classroom door (on advertising hoardings, on television, on street signs, etc.) and they need to learn how to handle them. The messages children receive from TV programmes can be amplified many times as they play with mass-produced models of the TV characters, read books about them, dress up as them or carry belongings about in bags printed with the characters' image. With all this in mind, some of the less offensive resources can, if carefully and sensitively handled by the adults, be a useful learning tool; children can be encouraged to discuss the mismatch there may be between the image and their experience, for example.

Publishers should be made aware of why certain resources are being rejected. Nursery workers need to write to publishers and manufacturers, explaining their dissatisfaction. Publishers are notoriously slow in responding to changing demands, and until good anti-sexist resources are nationally available nursery staff will have to rely on small co-operatives who have managed to produce resources or continue to make their own.

Photographs of children engaged in a range of activities can make attractive, stimulating books. Enlargements of photographs showing women engaged in non-stereotyped occupations can be made into puzzles. Clothes for dolls or imaginative role-play need not be rigidly stereotyped; e.g. a white coat can be used to dress a male nurse, a female doctor or a vet. Likewise, a dressing-up box full of frilly negligées and high heels is likely to encourage a specific type of role-play and give clear messages about who the clothes are really for. We must bear in mind too the way resources are used in the busy classroom. We need to reflect on our own reactions and involvement with toys and observe how children use them on their own.

No matter how deep our commitment to anti-sexism and anti-racism, our own childhood experiences can be most influential. These are likely to be experiences of growing up in a sexist society, a point illustrated by an actively anti-sexist mother:

> I was looking after my son, his lifelong friend L. (a boy also aged 6) and L.'s 4-year-old sister. I first sat with the boys and their deployment of toy soldiers, knights and a rudimentary cardboard castle. . . . I picked up a knight and felt that I didn't know what to do with it. . . . I then went over to the little girl, who was sitting with tiny dolls, a dolls' house and furniture. I picked up a doll and when I was playing was astonished by the sudden awareness that I *knew* what to say, I *knew* the fantasies, the words, the gestures. A surge of emotion overwhelmed me. I felt I was in touch with my childhood self.
>
> (Gender Rules OK 1978)

Lisa Serbin and colleagues (1978) have discovered how influential adults in the nursery can be in giving young children sex-stereotyped labels for activities and toys. In one class they asked teachers to introduce three new toys: a fishing set, sewing cards and a counting puzzle game. The teachers tended to introduce the fishing set with stories of 'going fishing with Daddy', and the sewing cards 'like when Mummy sews on a button'. More boys than girls were asked to demonstrate the fishing set, and more girls the sewing set. Serbin concluded that children readily learned whether a toy was 'sex appropriate' or 'inappropriate' from such introductions. The fact that nursery-school teachers introduce activities in this manner suggests that they are providing children with sex-stereotyped labels for them.

Serbin also found that an adult's presence in particular activities and with particular toys can be a 'powerful factor in determining children's activities'. Girls felt encouraged by the teacher's presence to go into areas that they had previously left unexplored, such as the building blocks and trucks. Boys ventured into the 'girls' area' – the doll corner – most especially when adults were there.

Once sensitized to the hidden, and often not so hidden, messages in visual images, nursery staff will be able to see for themselves changes they can make to their own nursery to ensure that sexist stereotyping is not being perpetuated.

'Unclouded minds'

Careful attention to the visual images in nurseries is merely one facet of anti-sexist provision. To ensure a non-sexist atmosphere that will encourage children to challenge sex stereotyping, nursery staff need to think carefully about the language they use; their expectations as regards behaviour and attitudes; the types of toys used and what it is hoped children will learn through playing with them; who visits the nursery and who helps in the nursery (is it always junior girls or secondary girls?). Nursery workers need to be aware of the forms of sexism and racism operating in society as a whole; then they can begin to develop strategies and resources that will enable children to challenge socially constructed sex- and race-based stereotypes and break free from their inhibiting influence.

Anti-sexist nursery provision is not about helping girls to

become more like boys by developing in them those skills and attributes many societies have prized for so long (e.g. aggression and competitiveness). It is concerned with recognizing the value to both girls and boys of 'feminine' attributes such as sensitivity and supportiveness and of 'masculine' attributes such as curiosity, assertiveness and resourcefulness. It also means helping children to see that adults around them value these attributes in everyone, regardless of sex.

We need to ensure that visual resources in nurseries do not present just one view of reality but, by drawing on the experiences and values of other women, ensure that children are presented with a balance of views of the world, which in turn reflect the diversity of the society in which they operate. Only when such a balance has been achieved will it be possible to suggest that, in nurseries, 'unclouded minds saw unclouded visions' (Riley 1985).

CHAPTER 9

Propagenda in the nursery

ANITA PRESTON

In order to counteract sexist practice, one first has to recognize it and distinguish it from other forms of oppression. Only then can it be dismantled. This chapter investigates ways in which anti-sexism, alongside and in partnership with anti-racism, can influence children's attitudes within the nursery and within the primary school.

Unless I want to refer specifically to a male, I will use the pronoun 'she'. In the context of this chapter, all the personnel in the nursery class who are seeking to establish egalitarian working relationships will be referred to as 'nursery workers'.[1]

Signals and strategies

If we walk into a school that is striving to be anti-sexist and anti-racist, what do we perceive? What evidence is there for the discerning and not so discerning eye? If the evidence does exist, does it appear to be there for the parents, the inspectorate, the staff, the governors, the children, the community? What are the signals, and could the strategies adopted be easily transferred to other school situations? Is there something in the *atmosphere* that can be sensed? Is it apparent, when we glide through a school with our antennae twitching, that we are in a building that facilitates, enables and encourages all within it to become more anti-sexist and anti-racist?

Not all that many years ago signs outside primary schools said, 'No parents beyond this point'; fortunately for all concerned, those unwelcoming signals, which served only to intimidate, have disappeared. In our school we have endeavoured to make the entrance more friendly by having a poster saying 'Welcome' in all the languages spoken by the children in our care. The staff have attempted to display an evenly balanced representation of gender and ethnicity and labelled the work in more than one language. The posters we use reflect the pulse of Hackney, and the information and leaflets are not about educational issues alone.

The literature immediately outside the nursery door and in the parents' room, and again on the second floor for parents of junior children, tackles abortion and divorce, head-lice and asbestos. We seek to advertise and consciously specialize in women's rights, employment, trade unionism, child care, maternity benefits, sexual harassment and legal injunctions. With the help of translators amongst our parents and staff and the GLC translation unit we reach all our parents by having the leaflets in many languages. We look for leaflets that are not limited to a strong heterosexist, white, nuclear-family orientation. Increasingly, libraries, women's groups, health clinics, crèches, etc. are doing the same.

We spent a good deal of energy setting up our parents' room and getting it into use. Some of the factors that influenced us were as follows. It had to be on the ground floor so that prams and push-chairs could be accommodated; it had to be near the loo for toddlers in tow; it had to have access to tea- and coffee-making facilities; and it had to be near the nursery for parents settling their children in. We wanted it to be cheerful, so we carpeted it. We made it more colourful with books, plants, pin-boards and fresh material. We wanted to ensure that our families would have somewhere to shelter from the rain, have a cup of tea and a chat, as well as possibly sign up for a language class or investigate the nature of the PTA. We wanted the parents' library, for example, to demystify the eduction process, point out the pros and cons of becoming a child-minder and help the parents to claim their rightful benefits. In short, we tried to create a supportive environment.

Taking our cue from the mothers we talked to, we recognized the need to consider the junior girls more sensitively. Were there bins or incinerators for sanitary towels? Did the children have to ask each time they needed a towel or could they help themselves? Who talks to the boys about menstruation, and how? We have only just begun to tackle this one, but it appears to be indicative of the confidence and strength of our parents that they could raise this issue in school.

Another area that has created more informality within the school and hence more friendships amongst the parents is the toy library. The Hackney Toy Library Association and a couple of members of staff worked very closely together before the toy library came into operation. Considerations from both sides included attempting to appeal to and excite children with gender-neutral equipment. By this we meant not using mass-produced television caricatures like Mr T. or the Incredible Hulk. We have omitted Barbie- and Cindy-type dolls and have instead a variety so that the children can choose an Afro-Caribbean, Oriental or Caucasian doll. The factors influencing the choice of toys were developmental *stages* rather than age, and a ban on weapons and aggressive toys. We wanted toys that excited, amused and challenged; and, particularly for girls, we wanted some of the traditional fare replaced. Just as we wouldn't dream of labelling water-play equipment as suitable just for boys or just for girls, dolls and Lego, cars and gardening implements equally have no such labels.

I have often noticed on visiting schools how evident people's roles are. When considering signals, indicators of anti-sexist work, a useful exercise is to watch the adults moving about the school and ask oneself questions like these:

- Are some in overalls and some not?
- Is the caretaker female; is the secretary male?
- Is the headteacher black; is the NNEB student Asian?
- Are the dinner helpers bilingual?
- How are the staff addressed? Is everyone called 'Miss', or do the parents and children have a *genuine* choice about what to call the staff?
- Are there first names on the doors?
- What is the overwhelming message to an outsider: 'Please knock' or 'Please come in'?

The whole-school approach

As feminist nursery workers we could not allow ourselves to be content with creating an anti-sexist, anti-racist nursery. Our children use the corridors and the staircases, the halls and the playgrounds, the museum and the library, and we encourage them to move around the school as productively at 3 years old as at 11. Children who attend nursery classes within primary schools have an added dimension. They can gain independence and poise slowly, when they are ready; assemblies, apparatus and lunchtime need not be the daunting, overwhelming experience they often are for children fresh from home. However, this also means that nursery workers have to take on board the staircases and the library! If we find ourselves hesitating over using a certain staircase or a particular room then we also have to tackle other staff and methods of working. We have, in short, to carry anti-sexist practice as far as we can.

After a demanding day, meeting the needs of twenty-five full-time children, talking to parents, consulting with staff, attending union meetings and supervising NNEB students, where and how do we find time for raising feminist issues? The answer has to be little by little. Anti-sexism cannot be achieved by ignoring gender issues. Asking oneself questions about various rooms in one's own school is a productive way of focusing on how much patriarchy lingers. If the library isn't bursting with books depicting active girls and caring boys this is because not enough have been written yet, but it doesn't have to end there. Junior children have already been on the receiving end of a great deal of media bias, but the fact that we are used to it does not mean that we have to tolerate it. By asking questions about the books in the library, for instance, we open up new ideas and ways of exploring the options for women and girls.

In our school we found the need for us all to confront our own sexism. We wanted to look at our own internalized sexist and racist attitudes, and to question where we were being tokenistic; it takes much more than a few exotic touches like celebrating Divali to wipe out years of oppression. We explored hitherto forbidden areas, like who does the washing-up in the staff room. We asked ourselves whether changing the order on registers was important or trivial. We found the need to take contradictory effects into account; does asking for a father's work phone-number, with a view to ringing him in the event of his child being sick, help him see his dual responsibility, or does it reduce the self-esteem of the mother regarding the role she feels most comfortable in?

Some discussions will take place on a whole-staff basis, some in small groups, some women only, some feminists only, some with female parents, some amongst nursery workers only. An initial core might begin in a consciousness-raising fashion; seeking the help of other feminists might make this easier. The group might broaden to include other staff in one's own school and beyond – in the division, in the union and in groups like the Women's Education Group,[2] expressly formed for solidarity and support. It takes time, confidence and continual reassessment before confrontation with male staff and parents can profitably take place. Each group would be wise to test the water before making firm decisions about association or disassociation with men.

Although a 'whole-school' policy is the most desirable,

unless and until the male members of staff prove that they want to be allies, they might as well be left out of the debate. In this connection, the following questions might be included in a check-list to reveal the stance of other staff members.

1 Do the men volunteer to run the crèche at meetings?
2 Do they prepare the refreshments at parents' evenings?
3 Are the male staff eager to timetable some of their activities in order to make time, space and resources available to facilitate the smooth running of the girls' group?
4 Does the headteacher, if male, take the initiatives of the women staff seriously?
5 Are the staff happy about spending money on an anti-sexist specialist?
6 Do the men at staff meetings *hear* the women, or do they make a pretence at listening?
7 Do the men actively campaign for meetings to cater for staff with children of their own?
8 Do they campaign for crèches at union meetings?
9 Do they campaign for holiday and after-school care, for play centres, for maternity and paternity rights?
10 Have they actively sought to prioritize anti-sexism?
11 Have they initiated any men-only meetings?
12 Has their language altered since anti-sexist initiatives began?

Many topics are not limited to classroom practice. Indeed, many lie outside the educational arena altogether. One key issue for us was the guilt feelings generated by society's ambivalence towards employed mothers. It didn't take us long to see that the 'biology is destiny' argument had nothing to do with our concerns.

In our school we have clubs one afternoon a week. We began to take a more careful look at the choices the children were making. Girls and boys appear to be more experimental; the boys are joining the knitting groups and the girls' football is flourishing. It will be necessary to assess as time goes on how profound the changes are.

The assertion question also needs tackling. Is it really women who need to adapt their behaviour? And can't we declare our desire for Peace? Can't the supporters of Peace tell the children, and the parents, that it is offensive to us if 'weapons' are brought into the school? We need to be positive about caring and nurturing attitudes and ready to congratulate ourselves on taking an emotional stance, on using our intuition and for dropping competitiveness in favour of co-operation. We ought to ask bluntly too whether the primary school helpers were willing to give up their tea-making power.

Language and literature

One central issue for attention is our language. Here we have to be fastidious, especially since all the research indicates we have very different ways of talking to girls and to boys – not to mention the fact that we attend more to the latter than to the former. What separates the women from the ladies and the ladies from the girls? What gives the lollipop person the right to call us 'love' or the police constable the right to call us 'dear' with impunity? Looking at language is to tread an endless road with countless by-ways: on the surface and at the subliminal level, at the level of 'old wives' tales' and 'mother-in-law jokes', from looking at feminine suffixes to the gender-loading of many labels.

Look at language, and your attention naturally shifts to literature – to nursery rhymes, legends, myths and fairy tales. Why do we cling on to our old favourites? Is it nostalgia, or are we not creative enough to replace them? Isn't this an indication of what men have done to women's literary talents through the ages?

In time the image of the blonde-passive-impotent-timid-princess-waiting-to-be-rescued will have to be rejected. It is as much a part of the dominant cultural heritage as white sugar is, and equally harmful. Traditional rhymes and images can have a use; they can be an excellent starting-point for a discussion and/or a writing exercise. 'When she was good, she was very, very good, and when she was bad she was horrid'; the 9-, 10- and 11-year-old girls know what to call her: 'stroppy', 'silly cow', 'right little madam', 'stupid bitch'. It does not take much to get them to see that these are male labels, and they soon mobilize their imaginations to create new rhymes and stories with exciting images and illustrations. Through this there emerges a greater sense of solidarity too.

New words can be experimented with, and children need not be exposed to sexist language. That this is not far-fetched is revealed by the serious consideration given to it by several sociolinguists (Lakoff 1975, Spender 1981, Cheshire 1985). It is worth trying to refer to a child as 'bold' or 'confident' rather than 'naughty', worth talking about behaviour being 'unacceptable' or 'not permitted'. Three-year-olds can grasp these terms; they just have to experience them more regularly.

The censorship of language or materials may appear to other staff and to some parents as too strong or 'over the top', but it must be pointed out to them that no one deserves to be ridiculed, ignored or merely tolerated. As feminist workers, we must protest at all continuing societal distortions. Confronting staff and/or parents, we have to insist: 'We have documented the problem and we require a response from policy-makers, teachers and students. We do not expect to remain invisible and unheard' (Spender 1982).

The developing child

One of the ways the whole staff can investigate an example of sexism is by looking carefully at the records of progress. Although the pedagogic jargon refers to the 'whole' child, we still tend to look at a child's progress in facets or parts of the whole. One such facet is labelled 'emotional develop-ment'. Let us, for a moment, suspend conventional male wisdom and raise the status of the so-called feminine traits of caring, sharing, being sensitive and generous, and give them a new heading: 'problem-solving'. Now let us apply this new framework to the caring activity of bathing a doll and ask a new set of questions:

- Does the child prepare the area in advance?
- Are the necessary materials – soap, flannel, towel, shampoo, fresh clothes, powder – all to hand?
- Is the room warm enough, and does the child know how to raise and lower the temperature?
- Is the child able to avoid getting soap in the doll's eyes?
- How do you answer the phone with a slippery doll in your arms?

It becomes almost scientific! Heaven forbid that we encourage our children to exhibit technique at the expense of caring; but, because women's work is trivialized by men, and because baby care (doll care) has been similarly trivialized, such activities have never been seen as problem-solving. Would it not be right, then, for the records of progress to document, alongside pre-reading skills, colour recognition and mathematical awareness, accomplishments in doll bathing?

To be sure, it is not 'mere common sense' to be able to juggle a pooey baby, a wooden spoon, a toddler in a tantrum, and still answer the door. It requires tact, diplomacy, perseverance, patience, humour, strength, muscle, originality, ingenuity – the list is endless. As feminist workers, we must create our own home/hospital/shop/take-away/hairdresser's/garage/caravan/laundry corners to tackle these real-life situations.

The Home Corner
The home corners in our nurseries have for too long been too bland, too moderate, too self-controlled. Home is about crying babies and wet nappies; it is about unemployed dads and mums with three jobs; it is about violent videos and the frustrations built up by sitting in the dole queue with

nothing to do. It no longer makes any sense to listen to children – young uninhibited children – talking about their dads hitting their mums or about their gran dying, without creating a truly non-taboo classroom structure as well. If the home corner is only an area where 'associative play', 'parallel play', 'egocentric play' and 'co-operative play' take place, then we have to look very seriously at our nursery training and our in-service work. Anti-sexist and anti-racist play deserve overall attention. They are not options that can be slotted in or tagged on to teacher-training or nursery-training courses.

The most lucid, articulate, sophisticated and caring conversations I have ever had with nursery children have been around the so-called 'taboo' areas. A great deal of feminist work can take place here, and the reason that these issues have long been considered 'controversial' is perhaps that they have received that label from men. Male teachers, male heads, male parents, male inspectors not always but often find it difficult to talk about babies vomiting, mums bleeding the dads hitting. This is because we haven't challenged the notion of patriarchal values. Undermining the mother's role, we have undermined the nursery worker's role and hence the role of the child in the home corner. They are the ones who juggle the baby, the spoon and the doorknob; we must ensure that the children have the props to do just that. Controversial issues in the home have to be faced; they can no longer remain invisible.

Equal opportunity has to be more than a principle espoused in the staff room or in the hallway on a piece of green-and-purple paper. The green-and-purpleness merely alert those who already read the signals; those who are colour-blind (men) will go on ignoring it. If Dad is hitting Mum, it will be witnessed and deeply felt by boy children as well as by girls. Three- and four-year-olds, regardless of sex, are scared when this happens. Boys must be enabled to play out their fears as well as some aggressions; girls must be enabled to play out their strengths as well as some fears.

Emotional Equality

The relations of domination and subordination between the sexes will continue to be reproduced unless we provide alternative strategies for the development of caring, competent adults. Boys of 3 and 4 can be tapped at source on the topic of feelings. All children, when they enter the nursery, however well prepared, feel vulnerable and insecure. Whatever else they may have going for them (wit, maturity, kindness, intelligence, sympathy, humour, independence, etc.), which they may exhibit later on, when they first arrive they are bewildered: it is a shock to the system. If parents find this difficult to empathize with, let them remember how they felt on their first day in a new job. This is often a fair and just tactic to use if a parent doesn't see the need to settle a child in.

The child who cries, who sits on my lap, who sucks her thumb or twiddles her hair, who can't eat her lunch, go to the toilet, manage a smile or speak a word, that child – girl or boy, black or white – is experiencing feelings of loss, confusion and, often, betrayal: betrayed by a parent who said it would be lovely. Laurie Lee vividly brought out this sense of betrayal and bewilderment, remembering his first day at school when he didn't get the present he thought he had been promised:

> They said they'd give me a present. . . . They said, 'You're Laurie Lee, ain't you? Well, just you sit there for the present.' I sat there all day but I never got it. I ain't going back there again!
>
> (1959)

Bewildered and confused, the child feels the need to be cared for, protected. If she feels reluctant and anxious, then that ought to be acknowledged, and nursery workers have long since seen the value of easing a child in gradually. What we seem to have failed at is enabling parents to see that their boys will gain from this demonstration of feeling. It is not harmful to them to show emotion. Abandoning feeling by the age of 3 or 4 is a downright shame, and yet too many parents – mothers as well as fathers – encourage their male children to 'stand up for themselves', 'stop crying', 'be a big man' and so on. The idea that only women feel ensures that future grown men are emotionally bereft.

Parents often have enormously high expectations of their children, particularly if the child is a boy; but even the most enthusiastic child will have moments of regression. Even when steps are taken gradually, reinforced by home visiting and weaning towards separation, staff still find children dismayed by apparatus and totally thrown by lunchtimes. The way we conduct ourselves and the attitude we take towards the children are crucial for their emotional growth. It is also important to tell the parents how the child's day has gone.

One way is to say 'Fine' and leave it at that; but it is better to say, for instance, 'John was scared today. He didn't want me to leave him and go into the garden, and he didn't want to watch *You and Me* with the other children. Here are his pants and trousers. I've only rinsed them – we could do with a washing-machine in this school.'

The message is very different: first, that it is all right to be scared; secondly, four-year-old boys do cry and wet their pants; thirdly, other kids wet their pants too – which is why a washing-machine is needed. There is no whispered double-talk for the child to accommodate. The nursery worker was straight: she said it was OK to be scared. Even where there is a conflict, where values collide as they do occasionally between parents and staff, the child knows where he stands with the nursery worker.

The feminist context

This emotional directness will reap even more rewards if the nursery worker is prepared to share her feelings. When we had a hospital corner in the nursery recently, there was much labour talk. We talked about pain, blood, injections, breathing, placentas. We played out a lot of our fears, including mine, for I was pregnant. Having a hospital corner did not just mean extending vocabulary ('stethoscope', 'thermometer', 'amniocentesis') or acting out symbolically; it involved sharing mutual understandings and preoccupations with other women. Full-time mothers who double as nurses by night may bring bandages and wooden spatulas in as props. What they also bring, however, is knowledge and expertise, which then extend beyond the nursery door to other pregnant mothers. The sharing of maternity and baby clothes as well as experiences seems to happen spontaneously.

When I had head-lice last year, along with half the children, mothers shared their own tried and tested remedies, and together we looked through each other's hair. This had little to do with winning parents' approval or with parents winning staff approval. It is about female solidarity and common understandings – that is, feminism – and is one of the reasons why nursery work is so rewarding. The demands, though great, are no more than mothers of young children face all the time. Cognizance of this is often frowned upon by educationalists and trade unionists who are fighting for 'professional recognition'. Feminist workers have to be aware of this dilemma – it certainly needs further discussion.

Another area where dilemmas and possible conflict may arise, depending upon which beret you are wearing, is where anti-sexism clashes with multiculturalism. Some feminists disapprove of challenging ethnically based cultural differences, but over some issues I feel it is necessary. I am angry when Jewish males pray, 'Blessed art Thou that I was not born a woman', when a Catholic male denies a woman access to birth control, when Muslims say, 'Men are superior to women on account of the qualities in which God has given them pre-eminence.' I am not ambivalent. I am angry about female circumcision, about male oppression and violence towards females being excused as an aspect of cultural tradition; I am angry that such violence occurs in most societies. I am angry about father–daughter rape. I am angry that there are so few women doctors, lawyers and electricians, so few dads who can change nappies as well as tyres.

However, feminists do have ways of tolerating some of the burden of that anger without it extinguishing other positive feelings. The answer lies largely in sharing and solidarity; in having leaflets readily available, and a book full of phone numbers with everything from Women's Aid and Rape Crisis to Gingerbread and Prisoners' Wives in it. Outside the nursery is where the mothers meet and talk, and even if they reject the content of the leaflets they will not reject the overtures being made. Family violence is as common as head-lice; it straddles all classes and all races, is as silenced as menstruation and bears all the attached stigma. Nevertheless it happens to us all.

The time is long overdue; real changes must start happening for the girls we teach. Anti-sexism is about much more than girls entering traditionally male occupations. We want changes that girls can witness tomorrow. Some of this is surprisingly simple, almost frighteningly so. Just as we place things we want children to see at *their* eye level, so we can with non-sexist materials. Likewise with our language and explanations. Imagine that children ceased to witness unequal power relationships; imagine they mimicked anti-sexist adults – then phrases like 'Just you wait until your father gets home' and 'If you do that again, I'll send you to Mr . . .' would cease to be threatening. We *can* help children conduct themselves in a variety of stances, postures and ways of interacting. They do not have only one option available to them.

If a boy prepares a meal in the home/take-away corner, don't marvel at it; it's no big deal. Don't call him a 'gem' or a 'good boy', for we don't normally give a second glance to a girl doing it. It is very harmful for children to replicate the model of nuclear family life if nuclear family life is about women servicing others all day long.

Choice of resources and activities

Nursery workers take enormous care in selecting equipment. We look for obvious merits like educational value, aesthetic appeal, versatility and practicality, and we attempt to create an overall environment which ensures that the quality of play is of a high standard. But what do we do while we wait for the educational catalogues to become non-sexist? Groups such as the Bilingual Under-Fives team have produced some excellent materials;[3] but if anti-sexism and anti-racism are going to be a much more integral part of the nursery, then we need to alert Galt, Lego, Playpeople, Arnold and the other manufacturers about their outdated toys.

This is where gender-neutral equipment has a large part to play. Scrubbing brushes, paint rollers, chamois leathers, ladders, garden trowels, soft brooms and stiff brushes, torches, clocks, padlocks and keys, watering cans, shoe polish and sandpaper are all tools that aid children's development. Girls don't have to *learn* to be assertive in these areas. Generally they feel very comfortable with a paint roller; Mum does the decorating at home, and the staff paint the shed at the nursery. It's the books that depict us twiddling our thumbs that need to catch up. Children do not label these tools by gender: a paintbrush is a paintbrush is a paintbrush. What they do notice as significant is where these tools are used – *outside*.

Outside play has always been an undervalued facet of nursery education. Some nursery workers still regard the supervision of outside play as just that – supervision. Lack of involvement and interest and their converse, enthusiasm and vigour, are very infectious. Mothers and nursery workers are too often *inside*. They are inside clearing up, preparing the dinner, running the bath-water. Meanwhile Dad – if there is one – is outside: outside washing the car, digging the path free of snow, building a wall. It is the father who suffers the most if ill or unemployed, where the role segregation has been very marked. Children love outdoor activities. Don't be afraid of the rain and snow and mud. Emphasize to the parents the importance of warm, non-restrictive clothing that they can get on and off independently. Girls will continue to 'preen' if that is what wins approval. Children dressed for the *work* of the day –

woodwork, cooking, hosing down the furniture, scrubbing the easel, laundering aprons and fixing hinges – will demonstrate anti-sexist play.

Camping and caravanning make good alternative outdoor aids for imaginative play. Providing children with props that can allow them to be more experimental with sex roles out of doors is a way of enabling a more flexible range of possibilities in areas which might feel more comfortable to them. Photographs of the children on display and made into books to take home are ways of reinforcing what we are trying to do. A boy in a Nigerian dress, a girl unblocking the drains or using a magnet to catch metal fish – such images captured in a photograph or, better still, on video are irresistible and will enliven an open day or evening. When parents express genuine surprise at what their children are capable of, we can take the opportunity to point out the way the children are working towards anti-sexist and anti-racist practice. Unless we take it this seriously, we are actually signalling tacit agreement with sexism and racism.

The transformation of attitudes

It makes little sense to have an ILEA policy statement on the walls, unless we intend to back it up with plans, strategies and policies of our own – and this involves the children and the parents. Parents know things about their children that we don't and they can share in the record-keeping. We can use this time to ask, for instance, 'Has Daniel bathed a doll competently yet?' or 'Is he spreading the butter on the toast OK these days? He had a lot of difficulty at first in the nursery.' If this seems odd or daunting, remember (especially when talking to parents of boys) that all children need help at becoming more gentle and caring. Learning how to do this is not 'soft' or retrogressive but enhancing. Mothers who do not feel positive about the educational value of pushing a pram – not running with it at thirty miles an hour – or being tender with a doll – not holding its head under water – can be asked whether they wouldn't prefer being married to someone who cared in that way.

If we teach boys that the world is theirs, that they don't have to exercise self-control but only control over others, that girls and women are too weak to protect themselves and are here to service males, then we are training them to become predators. If we teach girls that fear about being alone is acceptable, that weakness is a virtue and that passivity and compliance are to be welcomed, then we are training them to be sexual objects.

Talking to older girls in the school about these issues is valuable and rewarding. Justice and equality are profoundly felt at 10 and 11 years, and talking about discrimination against women in, say, recruitment to medical schools can be linked to their experiences in the playground to raise their consciousness considerably.

It is worth discussing with older girls how it feels to be 'out of step' with the norms. Being open and honest about the readjustments and contradictions that abide when confronting anti-sexist behaviour is very important. So is knowing that there are staff in the school whom they can talk to. We must also be there in a supportive way, as we would be for our colleagues, ready to hear each other out, often in earnest, sometimes in rage. In this context, taking back-copies of magazines like *Spare Rib* into school is also helpful. Girls can then identify with the activities of millions of real women; real women, like their mums and their teachers, have little time between work, home, children, shopping, friends, meetings and union activity to pee, let alone powder their noses. Beauty, when a focus for women's attention, divides and separates women from each other. Asking girls to write about this topic can be really illuminating.

Girls in school can take a closer look at women's rights if the literature is there, always available. Feminist teachers can point out that 'caring' is often a misused term; caring for one's aged, infirm and handicapped is not liberating and doesn't pay the rent. Parental participation, if it actually equals unpaid labour, is neither truly voluntary nor anti-sexist.

No parent would purposely or deliberately chip away at their daughter's self-esteem, stifle her energy or cripple her creativity. Yet all of us who are parents have been guilty of perpetuating, to a greater or lesser extent, the damaging effects of sex socialization. Sometimes we are misinformed, sometimes we are mistaken, sometimes we don't want to relinquish our power and sometimes we don't want to acknowledge that we are blocking her full potential or fulfilment. 'Conventional wisdom' demands that women live vicariously and not dangerously. The time has arrived for the girls to live fully and become competent human beings.

Contempt for women and girls cannot be allowed to continue in our schools. We must combat it and at the same time point out that the oppression which reduces the status of women also reduces the nature of men. Discussions of sexism are often greeted with either silence or tolerant smiles, as if the very raising of the issue were frivolous, not part of the serious business of teaching. However, sexism and the surrounding issues deserve as close an examination as racism. As in the case of racism, we need to take the intentional as seriously as the unintentional. Prejudice – often in the form of deeply ingrained habits, almost reflexes – is highly resistant to change, but the feminist must challenge ideologies that justify and preserve the status quo.

I hope that in writing this chapter I have been able to raise many questions; certainly writing it did so for me. It has not been my intention to give simple apparent solutions. I have touched on delicate, controversial and difficult issues and have tried to provoke interest and discussion rather than be instructional.

Notes

1. 'Nursery nurses in education nurseries are paid considerably less than teachers, indeed, they are the lowest paid qualified group in the

public sector and they have no promotion prospects whatsoever. This relates partly to the fact that since 1960 their training has been shorter and is also undertaken at an earlier age, but probably is a reflection of the view that they are principally concerned with the children's "care" and that their care is presumed to need less skill and to be less important than their education. It is unlikely that children can separate their needs in this way or feel that their care is less important than their education, so why do we?' (Aspinall 1984).

2. The Women's Education Group, based at the Women's Education Resource Centre in London, runs discussions and produces the magazine *GEN*.

3. Bilingual Under-Fives is an ILEA research project. It has produced learning materials and a set of video programmes.

BIBLIOGRAPHY

Ahmad, K. (1977a) *Family Life in Islam*. Islamic Foundation.

(1977b) *Islam: Basic Principles and Characteristics*. Islamic Foundation.

Amos, V. and Parmer, P. (1981) 'Resistances and Responses', in A. McRobbie and T. McCabe (eds.), *Feminism for Girls*. Routledge.

Arcana, J. (1983) *Every Mother's Son*. Women's Press.

Archer, J. (1978) 'Biological Explanations of Sex-Role Stereotypes' in J. Chetwynd and O. Hartnett (ed.), *The Sex Role System*. Routledge.

Aspinwall, K. (1984) *What Are Little Girls Made Of? What Are Little Boys Made Of?* NNEB.

Badawi, A. (1981) *The Muslim Woman's Dress*. Ta-Ha Publications.

Barclay, L. (1974) 'The Emergence of Vocational Expectations in Pre-School Children'. *Journal of Vocational Behaviour*, 4.

Bayliss, S. (1985) 'Spending Cuts Pose Threat to Nursery Schools'. *The Times Educational Supplement*, 4 January.

Bean, J. (1978) 'The Development of Pyschological Androgyny: Early Childhood Socialization', in B. Sprung (ed.), *Perspectives on Non-Sexist Early Childhood Education*. Teachers College Press.

Belotti, E. G. (1975) *Little Girls*. Writers' & Readers'.

Black, C. (1915) *Married Women's Work*. G. Bell.

Blackstone, T. (1971) *A Fair Start*. Allen Lane.

Bland, L. (1981) 'It's Only Human Nature' 'Sociobilogy and Sex Differences' in *Schooling & Culture*, 10, Summer. ILEA Cockpit Arts Workshop.

Board of Education (1905) *Report on Children Under Five in Public Elementary Schools*. HMSO.

(1907) Report by Consultative Committee.

Bottomley, A. *et al.* (1981) *The Cohabitation Handbook: A Woman's Guide to the Law*. Pluto.

Boulton, M. G. (1983) *On Being a Mother*. Tavistock.

Bourne, J. (1983) 'Towards an Anti-Racist Feminism'. *Race and Class*, xxv (1). Institute of Race Relations.

Bowlby, J. (1952) *Maternal Care and Mental Health*. World Health Organization.

(1953) *Childcare and the Growth of Love*. Penguin.

Bowman, B. (1978) 'Sexism and Racism in Education', in B. Sprung (ed.), *Non-Sexist Early Childhood Education*. Teachers' College Press, University of Columbia.

Brah, A. and Minhas, R. (1985) 'Structural Racism or Cultural Difference?', in G. Weiner (ed.), *Just a Bunch of Girls*. Open University Press.

Bronfenbrenner, U. (1974) *Two Worlds of Childhood*. Allen Lane.

Brown, G. and Harris, T. (1978) *Social Origins of Depression*. Tavistock.

Browne, A. (1984) *Willy the Wimp*. Julia MacRae.

Browne, N. and France, P. (1985) 'Only Cissies Wear Dresses', in G. Weiner (ed.), *Just a Bunch of Girls*. Open University Press.

Bruner, J. (1980) *Under Five in Britain*. Grant McIntyre.

Burns, J. (1906) *Report of the Proceedings of the National Conference on Infantile Mortality*. P. S. King and Co.

Buxbaum, E. (1951) *Your Child Makes Sense: A Guidebook for Parents*. Allen Lane.

Byrne, E. M. (1978) *Women and Education*. Tavistock.

Campbell, P. and Wirtenberg, J. (1978) 'How Books Influence Children'. *CIBC Bulletin*, 11 (6).

Carlsson, N. (1984) *Harriet and the Rollercoaster*. Picture Puffins.

CEC (1979) *Europeans and Their Children*. Eurostat Brussels.

CEC (1981) *Public Expenditure and Training*. Eurostat Luxembourg.

CERI (1977) *Early Childhood Care and Education*. Paris, OECD.

Chaney, J. (1981) *Social Networks and Job Information*. EOC/SSRC.

Cheshire, J. (1985) 'A Question of Masculine Bias'. *English Today*, 1, January. Cambridge University Press.

Clarricoates, K. (1980) 'The Importance of Being Ernest . . . Emma . . . Tom and Jane', in R. Deem (ed.), *Schooling for Women's Work*. Routledge.

Comer, L. (1974) *Wedlocked Women*. Feminist Books.

Coote, A. and Orbach, S. (1977) *Women's Rights*. Penguin.

CRC (1975) *Who Minds?* Community Relations Commission.

(1976) *As They See It*. Community Relations Commission.

Cunningham, J. and Curry, J. (1981) *The Babysitter Book*. Hamlyn.

Dally, A. (1982) *Inventing Motherhood*. Burnett Books.

David, M. (1985) *Critical Social Policy*, 12.

Day, C. (1975) *Company Day Nurseries*. IPM Information Report No. 18.

Deem, R. (1978) *Women and Schooling*. Routledge.

Dixon, B. (1977a) *Catching Them Young 1: Sex, Race and Class in Children's Fiction*. Pluto.

(1977b) *Catching Them Young 2: Political Ideas in Children's Literature*. Pluto.

Eichenbaum, L. and Orbach, S. (1984) *What Do Women Want?* Collins.

Eisenstadt, N. (1983) *Partnership Paper 2*. National Children's Bureau.

Equality for Children (1984) *Under Five and Under-Funded*. On Line Leisure Information.

Equal Opportunities Commission (1978) *I Want to Work but What about the Kids?* EOC.

(1984) *Submission to the Select Committee of European Communities of the House of Lords on the Proposed European Commission Directive on Parental Leave and Leave for Family Reasons*. EOC.

(1985) *Submission to the Department of Employment on the Amended Proposals for a Directive on Parental Leave and Leave for Family Reasons*. EOC.

Fairweather, H. (1976) 'Sex Differences in Cognition', in *Cognition*, 4.

Finch, J. (1984a) 'A First Class Environment?' *British Educational Research Journal*, 10 (1).

(1984b) *Journal of Social Policy London*, 13. 'The Deceipt of Self-Help: Pre-School Playgroups and Working Class Mothers.'

Foster, M. (1985) 'A Curriculum for All?', in G. Weiner (ed.), *Just a Bunch of Girls*. Open University Press.

Frost, S. (1981) *Daycare Campaign Kit*. Finer Joint Action Committee Publication.

Fryer, P. (1984) *Staying Power: Black People in Britain since 1504*. Pluto.

Gardner, P. (1984) *The Lost Elementary Schools of Victorian England*. Croom Helm.

Garland, C. and White, S. (1980) *Children and Day Nurseries*. Grant McIntyre.

'Gender Rules OK' (1978) *Humpty Dumpty Radical Psychology Magazine*, 9.

Goodall, P. (1981) 'Children's Books: A Feminist View'. *Schooling and Culture*, 10, Summer.

Gordon, ?. (1900) *Policing Immigration: Britain's Internal Controls*. Pluto.

Gordon, ?. and Newnham, ?. (1900) *Passports to Benefits: Racism in Social Security*. Runnymede Trust.

Goutard, M. (1979) *Pre-School Education in the European Community*. CEC Series no. 12.

Graham, H. (1984) *Women, Health and Family*. Harvester.

Greenberg, S. (1979) *Right from the Start: A Guide to Non-Sexist Child Rearing*. Houghton Mifflin.

Griffiths, D. and Saraga, E. (1979) 'Sex Differences and Cognitive Abilities: A Griffiths Field of Enquiry?' in O. Hartnett, G. Boden and M. Fuller (eds.), *Sex Role Stereotyping*. Tavistock.

Hadow Report (1933) Part III. HMSO.

Hansard. 12 June 1947; 28 May 1948; 24 April 1967. HMSO.

Hardyment, C. (1984) *Dream Babies*. Oxford University Press.

Hargreaves, R. (1981) *Little Miss Scatterbrain*. Thurman.

Hart, R. (1978) 'Sex Differences in Use of Outdoor Space', in B. Sprung (ed.), *Perspectives on Non-Sexist Early Childhood Education*. Teachers College Press.

Hemmings, S. (1980) 'What, Me Racist?' *Spare Rib*, 101.

Holly, L. (1982) 'Who's Holding the Baby?' *Spare Rib*, 122 Sept. 1982.

Hooks, B. (1982) *Ain't I a Woman: Black Women and Feminism*. Pluto.

Hull, Bell, Scott and Smith (eds.) (1982) *But some of us are brave, all the women are white, all the blacks are men?* Black Women's Studies/ Feminist Press.

Hunt, A. (1968) *Survey of Women's Employment*. HMSO.

Hutt, C. (1972) *Males and Females*. Penguin.

Hyde, G. D. M. (1978) *Education in Modern Egypt*. Routledge.

ILEA. (1982) *Equal Opportunities for Girls and Boys*. Report by the ILEA Inspectorate.

(1984) *Providing Equal Opportunities for Girls and Boys in Physical Education*. ILEA Study Group.

(1985a) *Improving Primary Schools*. ILEA.

(1985b) *Race, Sex and Class: A Policy for Equality*. ILEA.

Jackson, B. and Jackson, S. (1973) 'The Childminders'. *New Society*, 26, 29th November 1973.

Jackson, B. and Jackson, S. (1979) *Childminder*. Routledge.

Janssen-Jurreit, M. (1982) *Sexism: The Male Monopoly on History and Thought*. Pluto Press.

Jolly, H. and Gordon, H. (1982) *A–Z Pregnancy and Babycare*. Royal Society of Medicine.

Jones, L. (1983) *Keeping the Peace*. Women's Press.

Kobayash, T. (1976) *Society, Schools and Progress in Japan*. Pergamon.

Lakoff, R. (1975) *Language and Women's Place*. Harper & Row.

Leach, P. (1979) *Who Cares?* Penguin.

Lee, L. (1959) *Cider with Rosie*. Hogarth. Press.

Liddington, J. and Norris, J. (1984) *One Hand Tied Behind Us*. Virago.

Loo, C. and Wenar, C. (1971) 'Activity Level and Motor Inhibition'. *Child Development*, 42, 1971.

Mackie, L. (1985) 'Would Nannies have their Children Looked After this Way?' *Guardian*, 30th April 1985.

Maccoby, E. E. (1964) 'Effects of the Mass Media', in M. L. Hoffman and L. W. Hoffman (ed.), *Review of Child Development Research Vol. 1*. Russel Sage Foundation.

Maccoby, E. E. and Jacklin, C. N. (1974) *The Psychology of Sex Differences*. Stanford University Press.

Martin, J. and Roberts, C. (1984) *Women and Employment*. HMSO.

Massian, ?. (1900) *Women as Heads of Households in the Caribbean: Family Structure and Feminine Status*. HMSO.

Matlow, E. (1981) 'Advertizing, Imagery, Women and the Family', in *Schooling and Culture*, 10, Summer 1981. ILEA Cockpit Arts Workshop.

Mauger, P. *et al.* (1974) *Education in China*. Anglo-Chinese Educational Institute.

Mayall, B. and Petrie, P. (1983) *Childminding and Day Nurseries: What Kind of Care?* Heinemann Educational.

McArthur, L. and Eisen, S. V. (1976) 'Achievements of Male and Female Storybook Characters as Determinants of Achievement Behaviour by Boys and Girls'. *Journal of Personality and Social Psychology*, 33.

McGraw-Hill. (1974) *The McGraw-Hill Guidelines for Equal Treatment of the Sexes*. McGraw-Hill.

McRobbie, A. and McCabe, T. (1981) *Feminism for Girls. An Adventure Story*. Routledge.

Miller, C. and Swift, K. (1981) *The Handbook of Non-Sexist Writing for Writers, Editors and Speakers*. Women's Press.

Ministry of Education. (1946) *Not Yet Five* HMSO.

(1960) *Circular 8/60*. HMSO.

Ministry of Health. (1945) *Circular 221/45*. HMSO.

(1951) *Circular*. HMSO.

Ministry of Education. (1972) *Education: A Framework for Expansion.* HMSO.

Moraga, C. and Anzaldua, (eds.). (1981) *This Bridge Called My Back – Writings by Radical Women of Colour.* Persephone Press.

Moss, P. (1978) *Alternative Models of Group Childcare for Pre-School Children with Working Parents.* EOC.

Mottershead, P. (1978) *A Survey of Childcare for Pre-School Children with Working Parents.* EOC.

NAS/UWT. (1978) *Educational Provision for the Under-Fives.* NAS/UWT.

National Childcare Campaign. (1984) *Newsletter.* April–May.

New Statesman. (1984) 'Hiving off the Children', 17 August.

Oakley, A. (1976) *Housewife.* Penguin.

(1981) *Subject Women.* Fontana.

Penn, H. (1984) 'The Yugoslavian Way of Looking After Children'. *Guardian,* 2nd February 1984.

Perkins, E. and Morris, B. (1979) *Preparation for Parenthood: A Critique of the Concept.* Leverhulme Health Education Project, University of Nottingham.

Phillips, A. *et al.* (1983) *Your Body, Your Baby, Your Life. Guide to Pregnancy and Childbirth.* Pandora.

Piachand, D. (1984) *Round About 50 Hours a Week.* Child Poverty Action Group.

Pichault, C. (1984) *Daycare Facilities and Services for Children Under the Age of Three in the European Community.* OPEC.

Pierce, M. (1979) *Women on the Edge of Time.* Women's Press.

(1980) *Vida.* Women's Press.

(1982) *Circles on the Water.* Knopf.

(1983) *Braided Lives.* Penguin.

Pogrebin, L. (1982) 'I Have Seen the Future and It Almost Works'. *MS.*

Pole, T. (1823) *Observations Relative to Infant Schools.* London.

Price, R. (1979) *Education in Modern China.* Routledge.

Pringle, M. K. (1980) *The Needs of Children.* Hutchinson.

Queen, R. (1978) 'Towards Liberating Toys', in B. Sprung (ed.), *Perspectives on Non-Sexist Early Childhood Education.* Teachers' College Press, University of Columbia.

'Racism in Schools'. (1981) *Issues in Race and Education,* 34.

Rich, A. (1977) *Of Woman Born.* Virago.

Riley, D. (1983) *War in the Nursery.* Virago.

Riley, J. (1985) *The Unbelonging.* Women's Press.

Roberts, A. F. B. (1972) 'A New View of the Infant School Movement'. *British Journal of Educational Studies,* XX (2).

Roberts, R. (1977) *The Classic Slum.* Penguin.

Rodriguez-Trias, H. (1978) 'Problems and Priorities of Poor, Culturally Different Parents', in B. Sprung (ed.), *Perspectives on Non-Sexist Early Childhood Education.* Teachers' College Press University of Columbia.

Rowan, J. (1979) 'Psychic Celibacy in Men', in O. Hartnett, G. Boden and M. Fuller (eds.), (1979) *Sex Role Stereotyping*. Tavistock.

Serbin, L. (1978) 'Teachers, Peers and Play Preferences', in B. Spring (ed.), *Perspectives on Non-Sexist Early Childhood Education*. Teachers' College Press, University of Columbia.

Sherard, R. (1897) 'White Slaves of England', in P. Keating (ed.) (1978), *Into Unknown England*. Fontana.

Sivanandan, A. (1900) 'RAT and the Degradation of Black Struggle'. *Race and Class*, XXVI. Institute of Race Relations.

Smith, T. (1980) *Parents and Pre-School*. Grant McIntyre.

Spender, D. (1981) *Man Made Language*. Routledge.
   (1982a) *Women of Ideas and What Men Have Done to Them*. Routledge.
   (1982b) *Invisible Women*. Writers' & Readers'.

Spender, D. and Sarah, E. (eds.). (1980) *Learning to Lose: Sexism and Education*. Women's Press.

Spock, B. (1958) *Baby and Childcare*. Bodley Head.

Sprung, B. (ed.). (1978) *Perspective on Non-sexist Early Childhood Education*. Teachers' College Press, University of Columbia.

Stein, S. (1984) *Girls and Boys: The Limits of Non-Sexist Child Rearing*. Chatto.

Stones, M. (1981) *The Education of the Black Child in Britain*. Fontana.

Stones, R. (1983) *'Pour Out the Cocoa, Janet': Sexism in Children's Books*. Longman for Schools' Council.

Strachey, R. (1978) *The Cause: A Short History of the Women's Movement in Great Britain*. Virago.

Thompson, P. (1975) *The Edwardians: The Remaking of British Society*. Paladin.

Thompson, S. K. (1975) 'Gender Labels and Early Sex Role Development'. *Child Development*, 46, 2nd June 1975.

Thompson, T. (1972) 'Lost World of Childhood'. *New Society*, Oct. 5th 1972.

Tizard, B. and Hughes, M. (1984) *Young Children Learning*. Fontana.

Troyna, B. (1983) 'A Review of David Milner's *Children and Race*: Ten Years On'. *Multiracial Education*.

Van der Eyken, W. (1977) *The Pre-School Years*. Penguin.

Wagner, M. and Wagner, M. (1976) *The Danish Nation's Child Care System*. Westview Press.

Walker, A. (1982a) *Meridian*. Women's Press.
   (1982b) *You Can't Keep a Good Woman Down*. Women's Press.
   (1983) *The Colour Purple*. Women's Press.
   (1984) *In Love and Trouble*. Women's Press.

Weiner, G. (1985) 'Equal Opportunities, Feminism and Girls' Education', in G. Weiner (ed.), *Just a Bunch of Girls*. Open University Press.

Whitbread, N. (1972) *The Evolution of the Nursery–Infant School (1800–1970)*. Routledge.

Whyte, J. (1983) *Beyond the Wendy House: Sex Role Stereotyping in Primary Schools*. Longman for Schools' Council.

Wilderspin, S. (1824) *On the Importance of Educating the Infant Poor*. London.

Wilson, A. (1978) *Finding a Voice*. Virago.

Wilson, E. (1983) *What's to Be Done about Violence Against Women?* Penguin.

Wilson, G. *et al.* (1980) 'Childcare Shapes the Future'. *CIBC Bulletin*, 14 (728).

Wing, ?. (1900) *Worlds Apart: Women under Immigration and Nationality Law*. Pluto.

Winnicott, D. W. (1967) *The Child, the Family and the Outside World*. Penguin.

Wollstonecraft, H. (1792) *Vindication of the Rights of Women*. 1978 edn. Pelican Classics.

Wood, D. *et al.* (1980) *Working with the Under-Fives*. Grant McIntyre.

Contact Organizations and Resources

Advisory Centre for Education
18 Victoria Park Square
London E2 9PB

Concerned with all aspects of education as it affects children and parents. Produces a small magazine called *Where*.

Building Blocks Project
Castlemead Estate
The Rampway
Camberwell Road
London SE5

Committed to anti-sexism and anti-racism with under-fives.

Campaign Against Sexism and Sexual Oppression in
    Education
7 Pickwick Court
London SE9 4SA

Produces an excellent newsletter.

Centre for Urban Educational Studies
Robert Montefiore School
Underwood Road
London E1

An ILEA specialist teachers' centre and the base for the Bilingual Under-Fives Project. Non-sexist book-lists and a display of books in the library are available.

Council for Interracial Books for Children
1841 Broadway
Room 500
New York
NY 0023
USA

The CIBC's publications are well worth getting hold of. They include tape/slide presentations and a magazine, *Bulletin*.

Lambeth Toys
130/146 Ferndale Road
London SW4 7SB

A women's co-operative, which has produced toys for young children.

London Childcare Network
contact: Sue Hunter
8 Wakley Street
London EC1V 7QE

Committed to anti-sexist and anti-racist child care, the defence of existing provision and an opposition to all cuts. Produces a newsletter.

National Childcare Campaign
Wesley House
70 Great Queen Street
London WC2

Has several publications.

National Childminding Association
13 London Road
Bromley
Kent

National Children's Bureau
8 Wakley Street
London EC1V 7QE

National Committee on Racism in Children's Books
240 Lancaster Road
London W11

Produces an excellent magazine, *Dragon's Teeth* (subscription details from Ravi Jain, 46 High Street, Southall, Middlesex).

Women's Education Resource Centre
ILEA Tape and Drama Centre
Princeton Street
London WC1

Runs seminars and produces *GEN* magazine.

Women's Research and Resources Centre
190 Upper Street
London N1

Based above Sisterwrite bookshop.

Workplace Nurseries Campaign
Room 205
Southbank House
Black Prince Road
London SE1 7SJ

Bookshops
There are a growing number of bookshops that stock children's stories with a non-racist and non-sexist focus. Some of the above-mentioned organizations will be able to give an indication of appropriate addresses; otherwise contact:

Federation of Alternative Bookshops
c/o Mushroom
10 Heathcote Street
Nottingham NG1 3AA

Index